Completely Cookies

Also by Leslie Weiner and Barbara Albright
Mostly Muffins
Wild About Brownies
Simply Scones

Completely Cookies

Leslie Weiner and Barbara Albright

Illustrations by Diana Thewlis

ST. MARTIN'S PRESS ◆ NEW YORK

Library of Congress Cataloging-in-Publication Data

Weiner, Leslie.
     Completely cookies / Leslie Weiner and Barbara Albright.
         p.   cm.
     ISBN 0-312-05405-X
     1. Cookies.   I. Albright, Barbara.   II. Title.
TX772.W42   1991
641.8'654—dc20   90-49537
                                        CIP

First Edition: March 1991
10 9 8 7 6 5 4 3

To our editor, Barbara Anderson, for her patience.

To Lauren Jamie Weiner, who was in progress during the testing of our cookie recipes and was born June 27, 1990. (Do massive quantities of cookies consumed during pregnancy lead to colic?)

To Ted and Lowell, our tolerant husbands, who survived yet another cookbook.

To the game of golf, for keeping our husbands occupied while we worked on our book. The party is over, however, and we want you back.

Contents

Metric and Imperial Conversions

All of the recipes in *Completely Cookies* were tested using U.S. Customary measuring cups and spoons. Following are approximate conversions for weight and metric measurements. Results may vary slightly when using approximate conversions. Ingredients also vary from country to country. However, we wanted to include this list so you'll be able to make cookies wherever you may be.

◆ VOLUME CONVERSIONS ◆

U.S. Customary	Approximate Metric Conversion (ml)
⅛ teaspoon	0.5 ml
¼ teaspoon	1.0 ml
½ teaspoon	2.5 ml
1 teaspoon	5.0 ml
1 tablespoon (3 teaspoons)	15.0 ml
2 tablespoons	30.0 ml
3 tablespoons	45.0 ml
¼ cup (4 tablespoons)	60.0 ml
⅓ cup (5⅓ tablespoons)	79.0 ml
½ cup (8 tablespoons)	118.0 ml
⅔ cup (10⅔ tablespoons)	158.0 ml
¾ cup (12 tablespoons)	177.0 ml
1 cup	237.0 ml

◆ LENGTH CONVERSIONS ◆

U.S. Inches	Approximate Metric Conversion (cm)
⅜ inch	Scant 1 cm
½ inch	1.0 cm
⅝ inch	1.5 cm
1 inch	2.5 cm
2 inches	5.0 cm
3 inches	7.5 cm
4 inches	10.0 cm
5 inches	12.5 cm
6 inches	15.0 cm
7 inches	17.5 cm
8 inches	20.0 cm
9 inches	22.5 cm
10 inches	25.0 cm
11 inches	27.5 cm
12 inches	30.0 cm
13 inches	32.5 cm
14 inches	35.0 cm
15 inches	37.5 cm

◆ COMMONLY USED INGREDIENT CONVERSIONS ◆

ALL-PURPOSE FLOUR, UNSIFTED AND SPOONED INTO THE CUP

Volume	Ounces	Grams
¼ cup	1.1 oz	31 gm
⅓ cup	1.5 oz	42 gm
½ cup	2.2 oz	63 gm
1 cup	4.4 oz	125 gm

GRANULATED SUGAR

Volume	Ounces	Grams
1 teaspoon	.1 oz	4 gm
1 tablespoon	.4 oz	12 gm
¼ cup	1.8 oz	50 gm
⅓ cup	2.4 oz	67 gm
½ cup	3.5 oz	100 gm
1 cup	7.1 oz	200 gm

FIRMLY PACKED BROWN SUGAR

Volume	Ounces	Grams
1 tablespoon	.5 oz	14 gm
¼ cup	1.9 oz	55 gm
⅓ cup	2.6 oz	73 gm
½ cup	3.9 oz	110 gm
1 cup	7.8 oz	220 gm

UNSALTED BUTTER

Volume	Ounces	Grams
1 tablespoon	.5 oz	14 gm
¼ cup	2.0 oz	57 gm
⅓ cup	2.6 oz	76 gm
½ cup	4.0 oz	113 gm
1 cup	8.0 oz	227 gm

NUTS

Volume	Ounces	Grams
¼ cup	1.0 oz	28 gm
⅓ cup	1.3 oz	38 gm
½ cup	2.0 oz	57 gm
1 cup	4.0 oz	113 gm

♦ OVEN TEMPERATURE CONVERSIONS ♦

Fahrenheit	Approximate Celsius (Centigrade)
300°F.	150°C.
325°F.	160°C.
350°F.	175°C.
375°F.	190°C.
400°F.	200°C.
425°F.	220°C.
450°F.	230°C.

Completely Cookies

Introduction

You might be surprised to learn that this book originally started out as *Only Oats*. Along with the rest of the United States, we thought we wanted to climb aboard the oat bran wagon, but after completing about half the research for that book (and after a day of sampling twenty-seven different varieties of cooked oat products), we concluded that the bran wagon should go on without us.

We told our editor, Barbara Anderson, that whether oats were haute or not, and whether they were good for our hearts or not, we simply couldn't face another oatmeal meatloaf. When she asked what topic our taste buds could tolerate (and obviously the title had to end in "ly" as do the titles of our other two cookbooks—*Mostly Muffins* and *Simply Scones*), we put on our thinking caps. We considered *Absolutely Apples*, *Basically Bananas*, *Mainly Mushrooms*, and *Totally Tomatoes*, but the topic that most tempted our palates was cookies. We felt we could eat cookies on a daily basis for an extended period of time—a major requirement for creating any cookbook.

After many months of baking, burning, eating, tossing, and unloading literally thousands of cookies on our friends, we came up with this cookie collection. We lived to tell about it—and we still love cookies. We hope that you'll love the recipes that we selected, and hope that you'll use this book to keep your cookie jar completely filled.

BAKING

Before preparing cookies, read each recipe carefully, assemble the equipment, prepare the baking sheets, and measure the ingredients. This simple procedure (which holds true for all recipes) will help avoid many mishaps.

If the cookie dough needs to be chilled before shaping, you can save time by freezing it. And, if the dough becomes too soft to handle or shape, place it in the freezer for ten or fifteen minutes.

Preheat the oven to the specified temperature and check the temperature of your oven with an oven thermometer. (Mercury oven thermometers work best.) Oven temperatures vary, however, so check the cookies at the minimum baking time recommended in each recipe to avoid overbrowning, especially when trying recipes for the first time.

For best results, use good quality baking sheets and bake one sheet at a time, on the middle oven rack. Cookies baked on each sheet should be the same size and thickness so that they will cook evenly. Baking sheets should be cooled before reusing, because warm baking sheets may cause the dough to spread before baking. Instead of buttering baking sheets, you can line them with parchment paper for easy cleanup, or spray them with nonstick vegetable cooking spray. If your oven has hot spots, reverse the baking sheet halfway through baking for more even browning.

If you want to bake two sheets at once, make sure there is some room between oven racks. Place one baking sheet on an upper rack and one on a lower rack, but not directly under the first sheet. There should be space around the sheets for air circulation. Switch the positions of the sheets halfway through baking. Baking two sheets at a time may increase the cooking time slightly.

If cookies are overbaked, they will become too dry. If cookies are underbaked, they will be too soft.

Follow the recipe directions for cooling the cookies. This usually includes a short cooling period on the baking sheet to firm up the cookies slightly before removing them to a wire rack to cool completely. Cooling cookies on a wire rack with adequate air circulation will help prevent them from becoming soggy.

Sandwich cookies will not be as crisp as unfilled cookies. Once a cookie is filled, the moisture from the filling makes the cookie soft. For crisper cookies, serve them immediately after filling. When filling the cookies, select those with the most similar shapes and sizes to sandwich together.

MEASURING

Be sure to use the appropriate measuring cups for dry and liquid ingredients. Use measuring spoons instead of flatware. Level off measuring spoons and dry measuring cups with the flat edge of a spatula. Read measurements for liquid ingredients at eye level. (Refer to individual ingredients for specific measuring instructions.)

STORAGE

Cookies are best served shortly after they are baked, but most can be stored successfully. Be sure to cool the cookies completely before storing them in an airtight container. Many filled, moist, and frosted cookies should be refrigerated, especially in warm weather. Store soft and crispy cookies in separate containers. To store cookies for long periods of time, freeze them in airtight containers. (The length of storage for cookies, as well as cookie doughs, will depend on your freezer and the individual recipe.)

Firm doughs can be prepared ahead and baked later. Wrap the dough in plastic wrap, seal in airtight containers, and refrigerate for up to three days or freeze for up to six months. Thaw the dough in the refrigerator before baking. Be sure to label cookies and doughs with the type and date before freezing so that you do not have any mystery packages in your freezer. To save time, include baking instructions along with the frozen dough.

INGREDIENTS

FLOUR

Unless otherwise specified, the recipes call for all-purpose flour, as this is the type of flour that most people have on hand. To measure any type of flour, lightly spoon the flour into the appropriate dry measuring cup. Try not to be heavy-handed. Level it off with the straight edge of a knife. Do not tap the cup or dip it into the flour or you will end up with more flour than is needed. Even a small amount of extra flour can turn an otherwise moist and chewy cookie into a hard, dry cookie.

SUGAR

We've used granulated sugar, confectioners' sugar, and brown sugar in these recipes. In addition to adding sweetness, sugar is important to the texture of baked items. In our recipes we have used enough sugar to make good-tasting tender cookies, but they are not excessively sweet. Measure granulated sugar by filling the appropriate dry measuring cup. Level it off with the straight edge of a knife. Measure confectioners' sugar in the same way that you measure flour. Light and dark brown sugar are basically interchangeable in recipes. Dark brown sugar will produce darker cookies. To measure brown sugar, press it firmly into the appropriate-size dry measuring cup(s) until it is level with the top edge. It should hold the form of the cup when turned out.

Store brown sugar in airtight containers in a cool place. One manufacturer recommends freezing brown sugar for lengthy storage, and most manufacturers include softening directions on the package should your brown sugar become dry and rocklike. One recommended method is to place the brown sugar in an airtight plastic container, cover the surface of the sugar with a piece of plastic wrap, and top with a folded moist paper towel. Seal the container for eight to twelve hours before removing the towel.

Whether you've had to soften your brown sugar or not, we've found that it is a good idea to squeeze the brown sugar between your fingertips as you add it to the mixture to eliminate sugar clumps in the finished product.

BAKING POWDER AND BAKING SODA

These two items are not interchangeable. Use whichever is called for in the recipe. Use double-acting baking powder, which is the type most readily available. (We have noticed that a few single-acting baking powders have been sneaking onto grocers' shelves.)

Double-acting baking powder enables leavening to occur both at room temperature and during baking. It contains two acid components, calcium acid phosphate and sodium aluminum sulfate, along with an alkali component, sodium bicarbonate (baking soda), and cornstarch. Adding liquid to baking powder causes a chemical reaction between the acid and alkali, forming carbon dioxide and water. Leavening occurs when heat causes carbon dioxide gas to be released into the dough.

When acid ingredients (such as buttermilk, yogurt, sour cream, citrus, cranberries, and molasses) are used in baking, it is usually necessary to add baking soda (sodium bicarbonate—an alkali) to balance the acid-alkali ratio.

Make sure your baking powder and baking soda are fresh. They can lose their potency if stored past the expiration date or if moisture gets into the container.

SALT

Our recipes use very little salt and, when divided among the dozen or more cookies in each recipe, the amount of salt is minimal. Don't leave it out. We think you will find that just a little bit greatly enhances the flavor of most baked goods.

EGGS

Select large, uncracked eggs. Letting the eggs reach room temperature before use makes it easier to incorporate them into the dough, but do not let them stand at room temperature for more than two hours. Because of the potential danger of salmonella in raw eggs, it is not advisable to taste any mixture containing uncooked eggs.

We do not recommend trying to substitute egg whites for whole eggs in these cookie recipes, as this may alter the texture of the baked cookies.

BUTTER

Use unsalted (often called sweet) butter in these cookie recipes so that you can more accurately control the amount of salt in the recipe. The cookies will taste better, too. Salt acts as a preservative and may mask the flavor of butter that is past its prime. Unsalted butter has a shorter shelf life, so if you are keeping it for long periods of time, be sure to freeze it. You may substitute unsalted margarine. However, do not substitute vegetable oil and expect to get the same results.

HEAVY CREAM

Use heavy (also called whipping) cream. Do not substitute light cream or half and half. When whipping the cream for filling, use a small, deep, chilled bowl; chilled beaters; and cold heavy cream for best results.

VANILLA EXTRACT

Use the real thing for better tasting cookies. Vanilla adds a full rich flavor to most cookies and it often allows you to get by with a little less sugar.

SPICES

Store spices in airtight containers away from light and heat. Older spices may lose their potency, so it is a good idea to date your containers at the time of purchase.

DRIED FRUITS

Most of our cookie recipes call for dried fruits. Do not substitute chopped fresh fruits, as the added moisture may create very soggy, soft cookies.

PEANUT BUTTER

Use commercially prepared peanut butter in our recipes. The health-food-store variety may change the texture of the baked cookie and will produce runny fillings.

NUTS

It is a good idea to taste nuts before using them, as they can become rancid and spoil your cookies. Store nuts in airtight containers in the refrigerator or freezer. We like nuts and have used them in many recipes. If chopped nuts are stirred into the cookie dough, you can usually leave them out if you do not care for nuts. Remember, however, that the yield will decrease if you omit the nuts.

CHOCOLATE

It is important to use the type of chocolate that is specified in each recipe. However, you can usually safely substitute equal amounts of different types of chocolate chunks or chips that are stirred into the cookie dough.

Store chocolate in a cool dry place. Never store it in the refrigerator or freezer, unless your kitchen is unusually hot. The moisture from your refrigerator or freezer may cause the sugar in the chocolate to rise to the surface and form gray streaks.

Melting chocolate: Our recipes instruct you to melt chocolate in the top of a double boiler, but the microwave method is easier. Place coarsely chopped chocolate in a micro-wave-safe container and microwave at medium (50 percent) for 1½ to 4 minutes (depending on the amount of chocolate), until the chocolate turns shiny. Remove the container of chocolate from the microwave oven and stir the chocolate until it is completely melted. Take extra care with white and milk chocolate (stir them earlier), as the milk solids in these products make them more temperamental. Cool the melted chocolate until tepid before adding to cookie dough.

UNSWEETENED COCOA POWDER

There are basically two types of unsweetened cocoa powder—alkalized and nonalkalized. The former has been treated with an alkali to make it less acidic. It is often called "Dutch-processed" or "European-style." In our recipes we've used nonalkalized cocoa powder because we think it gives a richer, more robust chocolate flavor to baked items, and it is readily available. (Hershey's brown container of classic cocoa powder and Nestle's are both nonalkalized.) Measure cocoa powder the same way that you measure flour.

ARRIVING SAFELY

Homemade cookies are always a treat. To ensure that the recipient gets cookies instead of crumbs, here are some helpful hints on wrapping and shipping.

Select cookies that can withstand the rough handling of a trip and do not require refrigeration. Sturdy bars and soft drop cookies tend to travel best.

Pack the cookies in an attractive container or tin and include the recipes—or better yet, a copy of *Completely Cookies*—as a special treat. Jazz up plain boxes with festive wrapping paper.

Winter is the best time to send food. There are three major ways to ship: the U.S. Post Office, United Parcel Service (UPS), and Federal Express. Whenever you send food, mark the package with the words *perishable* and *fragile*. Be sure to label both the inside and outside of the box with the address in case the label is torn off.

For extra freshness, wrap each bar individually in foil or plastic wrap before packing it in a container. Wrap cookies in groups of similar types; avoid wrapping soft and crisp cookies together. Pack heavier bars at the bottom of the box. Pack the cookies close together so that they don't jostle around in transit. Use additional packing material to fill all spaces snugly. Make sure to insulate the top and bottom of the container with crumpled wax or tissue paper, plain popcorn, plastic bubble wrap, or plastic foam pellets to prevent jiggling. For extra padding, place the container of cookies in a larger container that has been filled with cushioning material. Check with the shipping service that you are using to see if they have any special requirements. For instance, UPS recommends using corrugated boxes secured with packing tape. Do not use string.

MAIL ORDER SOURCES

Dried Cherries:
Amon Orchards
7404 US 31 North
P.O. Box 1551
Traverse City, MI 49685
(616) 938-9160

American Spoon Foods, Inc.
1668 Clarion Avenue
P.O. Box 566
Petoskey, MI 49770-0566
(616) 347-9030 or (800) 222-5886

Hazelnuts:
Evonuk Oregon Hazelnuts
P.O. Box 7121
Eugene, OR 97401

Baking Equipment:
Maid of Scandinavia
3244 Raleigh Avenue
Minneapolis, MN 55416
(800) 328-6722

Basically Bars
and Brownies

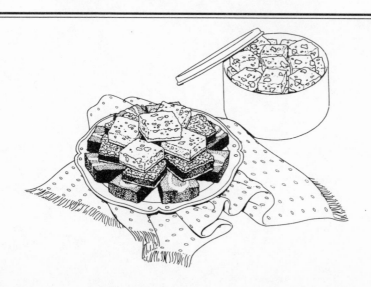

◆ APRICOT OAT BARS ◆

Oats, walnuts, and apricots complement each other very well in these moist and flavorful bars. Dried apricots are cooked in apricot nectar to give them extra flavor.

1½ cups finely chopped dried apricots
1½ cups apricot nectar
1½ cups uncooked old-fashioned rolled oats
1 cup all-purpose flour

½ cup chopped walnuts
⅛ teaspoon salt
½ cup unsalted butter, softened
¼ cup firmly packed light brown sugar
1 teaspoon vanilla extract

1. Preheat oven to 350°F. Line a 9-inch square baking pan with aluminum foil so that foil extends 2 inches beyond two opposite sides of the pan. Lightly butter the bottom and sides of the foil-lined pan.

2. In a small saucepan, over medium heat, cook apricots and apricot nectar for about 30 minutes, or until apricots are softened and nectar has almost completely evaporated and been absorbed. Remove pan from heat and cool.

3. In a large bowl, stir together oats, flour, nuts, and salt. In another large bowl, using a wooden spoon, cream together butter and sugar until combined. Stir in vanilla. Gradually beat in oat-flour mixture.

4. Firmly press all but 1 cup of mixture into bottom of prepared pan. Spread the surface with an even layer of the apricot mixture and sprinkle evenly with reserved oat mixture. Bake for 35 to 40 minutes, or until top is lightly browned.

5. Remove pan to a wire rack and cool completely. Using the two ends of the foil as handles, lift apricot "square" out of pan. Cut into rectangles. Store cooled bars in an airtight container.

Makes 12 bars

• CHOCOLATE CHIP BLONDIES •

Blondies are an all-American favorite. These are the perfect sturdy bars to tuck into lunch boxes for kids of all ages. They are also good for sending to faraway friends and relatives.

2 cups all-purpose flour
2 teaspoons baking powder
¼ teaspoon salt
½ cup unsalted butter, softened
1 cup firmly packed dark brown sugar

½ cup granulated sugar
2 large eggs, at room temperature
2 teaspoons vanilla extract
2 cups semisweet chocolate chips
1½ cups coarsely chopped walnuts

1. Preheat oven to 350°F. Line a 13-by-9-inch baking pan with aluminum foil so that foil extends 2 inches beyond the two long sides of the pan. Lightly butter bottom and sides of pan.

2. In a medium bowl, stir together flour, baking powder, and salt. In a large bowl, using a hand-held electric mixer set at medium-high speed, beat butter and sugars until combined. One at a time, beat in eggs, beating well after each addition. Beat in vanilla. With mixer on low speed, beat in flour mixture just until combined. Using a wooden spoon, stir in chocolate chips and nuts.

3. Scrape batter into prepared pan and smooth surface with a rubber spatula. Bake for 22 to 27 minutes, or until top is golden brown and blondies are set. Do not overbake.

4. Remove pan to a wire rack and cool for 30 minutes. Using the two ends of the foil as handles, lift chocolate chip "rectangle" out of pan. Cool on foil for at least 2 hours and cut into bars.

These blondies freeze well.

Makes 24 blondies

• CHOCOLATE CHUNK OAT BARS •

These bars make perfect lunch box additions or after school snacks.

1 cup all-purpose flour
1 cup uncooked old-fashioned rolled oats
2 teaspoons baking powder
1/2 teaspoon salt
1/2 cup unsalted butter, softened
3/4 cup firmly packed light brown sugar
1/2 cup granulated sugar
1/4 cup light corn syrup

2 large eggs, at room temperature
2 teaspoons vanilla extract
6 ounces bittersweet chocolate, cut into
1/2-inch chunks
6 ounces milk chocolate, cut into 1/2-inch
chunks
1 cup coarsely chopped walnuts or pecans

1. Preheat oven to 350°F. Line a 13-by-9-inch baking pan with aluminum foil so that foil extends 2 inches beyond two long sides of pan. Lightly butter bottom and sides of foil-lined pan.

2. In a large bowl, stir together flour, oats, baking powder, and salt. In another large bowl, using a hand-held electric mixer set at medium speed, beat butter, sugars, and corn syrup for 1 to 2 minutes, until combined. One at a time, beat in eggs, beating well after each addition. Beat in vanilla. With mixer on low speed, add oat-flour mixture and beat just until combined. Using a wooden spoon, stir in chocolates and nuts.

3. Scrape batter into prepared pan and smooth top with a rubber spatula. Bake for 33 to 37 minutes, or until the top is golden brown and bars are set. Do not overbake.

4. Remove pan to a wire rack and cool for 30 minutes. Using the two ends of the foil as handles, lift chocolate chunk oat "rectangle" out of pan. Cool on foil for at least 2 hours and cut into bars. Store cooled bars in an airtight container.

These bars freeze well.

Makes 24 bars

• FRAMBOISE BROWNIES •

Raspberry and chocolate were made for each other. These chocolaty brownies are a perfect example. Try a large square topped with a scoop of vanilla ice cream, chocolate sauce, and a garnish of fresh raspberries for a wickedly delicious dessert. Make sure to use the rosy-colored framboise (raspberry brandy) in the brownie recipe. If you want a more intense raspberry flavor, brush the top of the brownies with an additional tablespoon of framboise after they are baked and have cooled for 30 minutes.

1 cup unsalted butter, cut into tablespoons
12 ounces bittersweet chocolate, coarsely
 chopped
2 ounces unsweetened chocolate, coarsely
 chopped
¾ cup granulated sugar

¾ cup firmly packed dark brown sugar
3 large eggs, at room temperature
½ cup framboise
2 teaspoons vanilla extract
1¼ cups all-purpose flour
¼ teaspoon salt

1. Preheat oven to 350°F. Line a 13-by-9-inch baking pan with aluminum foil so that foil extends 2 inches beyond two long sides of the pan. Lightly butter bottom and sides of foil-lined pan.

2. In the top of a double boiler, over hot, not simmering, water, melt butter and chocolates, stirring occasionally, until smooth. Remove top part of double boiler from bottom and cool chocolate for about 10 minutes, or until tepid.

3. In a large bowl, using a hand-held electric mixer set at high speed, beat sugars and eggs for 4 to 5 minutes, or until mixture thickens and is light-colored. Beat in framboise and vanilla. Beat in cooled chocolate mixture until well combined. With mixer on low speed, beat in flour and salt just until mixed.

4.   Scrape batter into prepared pan and smooth surface with a rubber spatula. Bake for 25 to 30 minutes, or until a cake tester or toothpick inserted 2 inches from center comes out slightly moist. Do not overbake.

5.   Remove pan to a wire rack and cool completely. Using the two ends of the foil as handles, lift framboise "rectangle" out of pan. Cut into bars.

These brownies freeze well.

Makes 20 brownies

Rich and crunchy, these are sure to please kids of any age.

2⅓ cups uncooked old-fashioned rolled
   oats
2 tablespoons oat bran
2 tablespoons honey-crunch wheat germ
2 tablespoons sesame seeds
¼ cup slivered almonds
¼ cup coarsely chopped walnuts or
   pecans
¼ cup vegetable oil
¼ cup honey

⅛ teaspoon salt (optional)
1 teaspoon vanilla extract
1 cup crisped rice cereal
3 tablespoons light corn syrup
½ cup chopped dried apricots
⅓ cup raisins
1 bar (3 ounces) white chocolate,
   chopped, or ½ cup white chocolate
   chips

1.   Preheat oven to 350°F. Lightly oil a 15-by-10-inch jelly roll pan. Lightly grease a 9-inch square baking pan. Line square pan with aluminum foil so that foil extends 2 inches beyond opposite sides of pan. Lightly butter bottom and sides of foil-lined pan.

2.   In a large bowl, combine oats, bran, wheat germ, sesame seeds, and nuts.

3.   In a 3-quart saucepan, combine oil, honey, and salt (if desired). Cook over medium-high heat, stirring often, until mixture comes to a boil. Remove pan from heat and stir in vanilla.

4.   Add oats mixture to saucepan and stir to coat. Spread mixture in an even layer on prepared jelly roll pan. Bake for 13 to 18 minutes, or until golden brown, stirring twice during baking. Keep oven set at 350°F.

5.   Carefully transfer hot granola to a large bowl. Immediately stir in rice cereal. Quickly stir in corn syrup until mixture is lightly coated. Stir in dried apricots and raisins. Stir in white chocolate until evenly distributed (the chocolate will melt).

6.   Using the bottom of a pancake turner, pack mixture into prepared square baking pan. Bake for 15 minutes, or until top is dry. Do not overbake.

7.   Remove pan to a wire rack and cool for 45 minutes. Using the two ends of the foil as handles, lift fruit and nut "square" out of pan. Cool on wire rack for 30 minutes. Invert and carefully peel off foil. Invert again onto a cutting board. With a large serrated knife, carefully cut into squares.

Makes 16 bars

• LAYERED TRIPLE CHOCOLATE OAT BARS •

This is a new, slightly upscale version of an oldie but super-easy goodie. Commonly called "seven-layer bars," "monster bars," "magic cookie bars," or "hello dollies," they are irresistible no matter what name you use for them. Even the most snobbish connoisseur will have trouble keeping a hand out of the cookie jar!

½ cup unsalted butter
1 cup uncooked quick-cooking rolled oats
1 cup graham cracker crumbs
1 can (14 ounces) sweetened condensed milk
6 ounces milk chocolate, cut into ¼-inch pieces (or 1 cup milk chocolate chips)

6 ounces bittersweet chocolate, cut into ¼-inch pieces (or 1 cup semisweet chocolate chips)
6 ounces white chocolate, cut into ¼-inch pieces (or 1 cup white chocolate chips)
1⅓ cups sweetened flaked coconut
1 cup chopped walnuts

1.   Preheat oven to 350°F. Place butter in a 13-by-9-inch baking pan and place pan in oven for 5 to 7 minutes, or until butter is melted.

2.   In a medium bowl, stir together oats and graham cracker crumbs and sprinkle mixture evenly over melted butter. Pour sweetened condensed milk evenly over crumbs. Sprinkle surface evenly with milk, bittersweet, and white chocolates, then with coconut and walnuts. Press down firmly. Bake for 25 to 30 minutes, or until lightly browned.

3.   Remove pan to a wire rack and cool completely. Cut into bars. Store cooled bars in an airtight container.

Makes 32 bars

For Layered Fruit and Nut Oat Bars: Preheat oven and prepare crust with butter, rolled oats, and graham cracker crumbs as directed above. Sprinkle crust with 1 cup broken walnuts, 1 cup broken pecans, and ½ cup slivered almonds. Pour 1 can (14 ounces) sweetened condensed milk evenly over nuts. Sprinkle surface evenly with 1 cup chopped dried pineapple, 1 cup chopped dried apricots, and ½ cup chopped pitted dates. Sprinkle evenly with 1 cup sweetened flaked coconut. Press down firmly. Bake for 22 to 27 minutes, or until lightly browned. Cool completely on a wire rack. Cut into bars.

Makes 32 bars

• MARBLED CREAM CHEESE BROWNIES •

This version of marbled brownies has an extra generous layer of a cream cheese mixture swirled through the rich fudgy brownie base.

6 ounces bittersweet chocolate, coarsely chopped
2 ounces unsweetened chocolate, coarsely chopped
16 ounces cream cheese, softened
2 cups granulated sugar, divided

4 large eggs, at room temperature
1 tablespoon vanilla extract, divided
1 cup unsalted butter, softened
1 cup all-purpose flour
¼ teaspoon salt

1.   Preheat oven to 350°F. Line a 13-by-9-inch baking pan with aluminum foil so that foil extends 2 inches beyond the two long sides of pan. Lightly butter bottom sides of foil-lined pan.

2.   In the top of a double boiler over hot, not simmering, water, melt chocolates, stirring often, until smooth. Remove top part of double boiler from bottom and cool chocolate until tepid.

3.   In a large bowl, using a hand-held electric mixer set at medium speed, beat together cream cheese and ⅓ cup of sugar until smooth. Beat in 1 egg and 1 teaspoon of vanilla until combined. Set aside.

4.   In another large bowl, using a hand-held electric mixer set at medium speed, beat butter and remaining 1⅔ cups sugar until combined. One at a time, beat in remaining 3 eggs, beating well after each addition. Beat in melted chocolate and remaining 2 teaspoons vanilla extract. With mixer on low speed, beat in flour and salt just until combined.

5.   Scrape all but 1 cup of chocolate batter into prepared pan and smooth top with a rubber spatula. Spread cream cheese mixture evenly over batter. Spoon reserved chocolate batter over cream cheese mixture. Pull a table knife through the layers of batter in a zigzag fashion to create a marbled effect. Bake for 33 to 38 minutes, or until a cake tester or toothpick inserted 2 inches from center comes out slightly moist.

6.   Remove pan to a wire rack and cool completely. Using the two ends of the foil as handles, lift marbled cream cheese "rectangle" out of pan. Cut into bars. Store bars in an airtight container in refrigerator.

Makes 20 bars

• MIXED NUT PIE BARS •

With its combination of pecans, walnuts, almonds, and peanuts, this is like a pecan pie in bar form.

CRUST
1¼ cups all-purpose flour
2 tablespoons firmly packed light brown sugar

⅛ teaspoon salt
⅓ cup unsalted butter, softened

NUT TOPPING
½ cup dark corn syrup
¼ cup real maple syrup
¼ cup firmly packed light brown sugar
2 tablespoons unsalted butter, melted
3 large eggs, at room temperature
1 teaspoon vanilla extract

3 tablespoons all-purpose flour
⅛ teaspoon salt
½ cup chopped pecans (see Note)
½ cup chopped walnuts
¼ cup slivered almonds
¼ cup unsalted peanuts

1. *To prepare crust:* Preheat oven to 350°F. Lightly butter a 9-inch square baking pan. Line pan with aluminum foil so that foil extends 2 inches beyond two opposite sides of pan. Fold overhanging ends down along outside of pan. Butter bottom and sides of foil-lined pan.

2. In a large bowl, stir together flour, brown sugar, and salt. Work in softened butter until combined. Press dough into bottom and ¼ inch up sides of prepared baking pan. Bake for 15 minutes, or until very lightly browned.

3. Remove pan to a wire rack and cool for 15 minutes.

1. *To prepare topping:* In a large bowl, using a fork, stir together corn syrup, maple syrup, brown sugar, and butter until combined. One at a time, stir in eggs, stirring well after each addition. Stir in vanilla, then flour and salt, until blended. Stir in nuts. Pour mixture over cooled crust. Bake for 35 to 40 minutes, or until a knife inserted in the center comes out clean.

2. Remove pan to a wire rack and let it stand for 2½ hours, or until completely cooled. Using the two ends of the foil as handles, lift the mixed nut pie "square" out of the pan and invert onto a cutting board. Invert again onto a wire rack so that cookies are right side up, and cool for 30 minutes. Remove to a cutting board. Using a long serrated knife, cut into bars, wiping knife clean between each cutting. Place bars on wire rack and cool completely. Store bars in an airtight container in refrigerator. Serve at room temperature.

Makes 16 bars

Note: Any combination of nuts totaling 1½ cups can be substituted.

• OAT-BOTTOMED BROWNIES •

These rich, fudgy brownies are definitely decadent. An optional oat base adds chewy textural contrast. Mixing the ingredients in a food processor makes these bars extra speedy and eliminates the traditional brownie-making worry of scorching the chocolate.

OAT BASE

2 cups uncooked old-fashioned rolled oats
¾ cup all-purpose flour
½ cup firmly packed dark brown sugar

¼ teaspoon baking powder
⅛ teaspoon salt
⅔ cup unsalted butter, melted

BROWNIES

1 cup unsalted butter
¾ cup firmly packed dark brown sugar
¾ cup granulated sugar
18 ounces bittersweet chocolate, broken
    into pieces
2 ounces unsweetened chocolate, coarsely
    chopped

4 large eggs
1 tablespoon vanilla extract
1 cup all-purpose flour
¼ teaspoon salt
2 cups walnut pieces

1. Preheat oven to 350°F. Line a 13-by-9-inch baking pan with aluminum foil so that foil extends 2 inches beyond two long sides of pan. Lightly butter bottom and sides of foil-lined pan.

2. *To prepare oat base:* In a large bowl, stir together oats, flour, brown sugar, baking powder, and salt. Stir in melted butter. Firmly press mixture into bottom of prepared pan and bake for 10 minutes. Leave oven set at 350°F.

3. *To prepare brownies:* In a medium saucepan, combine butter and sugars. Heat over medium heat for 4 to 6 minutes, stirring frequently, until the butter is melted. In the container of a food processor fitted with the steel blade, process chocolates for 15 to 20 seconds until finely chopped. Add hot butter-sugar mixture and process for 15 to 20 seconds, until smooth, scraping down sides of work bowl as necessary. Add eggs and vanilla and process for 10 to 15 seconds, until combined. Add flour and salt and process for 5 to 7 seconds, just to combine, scraping down sides of work bowl as necessary. Add walnut pieces and pulse about 15 to 20 times to incorporate them into mixture and to chop them slightly.

4. Scrape batter onto baked oat base and smooth top with spatula. Bake for 40 to 45 minutes, until a cake tester inserted 2 inches away from center comes out slightly moist. Do not overbake.

5. Remove pan to a wire rack and cool for 2 minutes. Using the two ends of the foil as handles, lift oat-bottomed "rectangle" out of pan and cool on the foil for at least 2 hours before cutting into bars. Store the brownies in an airtight container.

Makes 20 brownies

◆ PEANUT BUTTER CHOCOLATE MALT BARS ◆

In this recipe, a cookie base flavored with malted milk is topped with the classic combination of peanut butter and chocolate.

COOKIE CRUST

1¼ cups all-purpose flour	½ cup unsalted butter, softened
⅔ cup malted milk powder	⅓ cup granulated sugar
½ teaspoon baking powder	1 large egg, at room temperature
⅛ teaspoon salt	

TOPPING

1 cup creamy peanut butter	¼ cup confectioners' sugar
2 tablespoons unsalted butter, softened	1 cup semisweet or milk chocolate chips

1. *To prepare cookie crust:* Lightly butter bottom and sides of a 9-inch square baking pan. Dust bottom and sides with flour and tap out excess.

2. In a medium bowl, stir together flour, malted milk powder, baking powder, and salt. In a large bowl and using a wooden spoon, cream together butter and sugar until combined. Stir in egg until blended. Gradually stir in flour mixture until combined. Cover and refrigerate for 1 hour.

3. Preheat oven to 375°F. Pat dough into prepared baking pan. Bake for 20 to 25 minutes, or until a cake tester inserted in center comes out clean and top is lightly browned. Remove pan to a wire rack and cool for 45 minutes.

4. *To prepare topping:* In a small bowl and using a fork, beat together peanut butter and butter until smooth. Beat in confectioners' sugar. Cover and refrigerate for about 45 minutes.

5. Preheat oven to 375°F. When crust is cool, spread peanut butter mixture evenly over crust. Sprinkle with chocolate chips. Bake for 3 minutes or until chips are melted. Using a small metal spatula, spread to a smooth layer. Cool slightly and refrigerate pan for 1 to 2 hours, or until firm. Cut into bars.

Makes 36 bars

◆ PEANUT BUTTER AND WHITE CHOCOLATE BARS ◆

Sweet white chocolate goes well with peanut butter, as do other chocolates! Try these bars with bittersweet, milk, or semisweet chocolate for other variations.

⅔ cup chunky peanut butter
¼ cup unsalted butter, softened
1½ cups firmly packed dark brown sugar
3 large eggs, at room temperature
2 teaspoons vanilla extract
1½ cups all-purpose flour

¼ teaspoon salt
1½ cups white chocolate chips or 9
  ounces white chocolate, cut into
  ¼-inch pieces
1½ cups peanut butter chips

1. Preheat oven to 350°F. Line a 13-by-9-inch baking pan with aluminum foil so that foil extends 2 inches beyond two long sides of pan. Lightly butter bottom and sides of foil-lined pan.

2. In a large bowl, using a hand-held electric mixer set at medium speed, beat peanut butter, butter, and sugar until combined. One at a time, beat in eggs, beating well after each addition. Beat in vanilla. With mixer on low speed, beat in flour and salt just until combined. Stir in white chocolate and peanut butter chips.

3. Scrape batter into prepared pan and smooth top with a rubber spatula. Bake for 20 to 25 minutes, or until a cake tester or toothpick inserted 2 inches from the center comes out moist. Do not overbake.

4. Remove pan to a wire rack until completely cooled. Then, using the two ends of the foil as handles, lift peanut butter and white chocolate "rectangle" out of pan. Cut into bars. Store bars in an airtight container.

These bars freeze well.

Makes 20 bars

◆ FIG OAT BARS ◆

Chock-full of fruit and nuts, these chewy, rich bars make great snacks.

2 cups uncooked old-fashioned rolled oats
1 cup all-purpose flour
1 teaspoon baking powder
¼ teaspoon salt
½ cup firmly packed dark brown sugar
½ cup unsalted butter, softened

2 tablespoons light or dark corn syrup
1 tablespoon molasses
1 large egg, at room temperature
1 teaspoon vanilla extract
1 cup chopped trimmed Mission figs
½ cup chopped walnuts

1. Preheat oven to 350°F. Grease bottom and sides of a 9-inch square baking pan. Line pan with aluminum foil so that foil extends 2 inches beyond two opposite sides of pan. Lightly butter bottom and sides of foil-lined pan.

2. In a large bowl, stir together oats, flour, baking powder, and salt. In another bowl, using a wooden spoon, cream together sugar and butter until combined. Stir in corn syrup and molasses until smooth. Stir in egg until blended, then stir in vanilla. Gradually stir in oat mixture until combined. Using a wooden spoon, stir in figs and nuts.

3. Scrape mixture into prepared pan and spread to an even layer. Bake for 27 to 35 minutes, or until the top is browned.

4. Remove pan to a wire rack and cool for 15 minutes. Using the two ends of the foil as handles, carefully remove fig oat "square" to the wire rack to cool for 30 minutes, or until firm enough to slide from the foil onto the rack. Cool on the rack for at least 30 minutes longer. Cut into bars.

These bars freeze well.

Makes 16 bars

Drop Cookies

◆ APRICOT WHITE CHOCOLATE CHUNK COOKIES ◆

Tart dried apricots are the perfect complement for the white chocolate in these crunchy oat cookies.

1¼ cups all-purpose flour
1 teaspoon baking powder
¼ teaspoon salt
14 tablespoons unsalted butter, softened
½ cup firmly packed light brown sugar
½ cup granulated sugar
1 large egg, at room temperature
1 teaspoon vanilla extract

2½ cups uncooked old-fashioned rolled oats
1 bar (3 ounces) white chocolate, cut into chunks, or 3 ounces white chocolate chips
½ cup chopped dried apricots
½ cup coarsely chopped pecans

1. Preheat oven to 375°F. Lightly butter several baking sheets. In a large bowl, stir together flour, baking powder, and salt. In another bowl, using a wooden spoon, cream together butter and sugars until combined. Stir in egg until blended. Stir in vanilla. Gradually stir in flour mixture until combined. Stir in oats. Stir in chocolate, dried apricots, and nuts.

2. Drop dough by rounded tablespoonfuls onto prepared baking sheets, leaving about 2 inches between rounds. Flatten slightly. Bake one sheet at a time, for 9 to 12 minutes, or until bottoms of cookies are lightly browned. Remove baking sheet to a wire rack to cool for about 2 minutes. Using a metal spatula, transfer cookies to wire racks and cool completely. Repeat until all dough is used. When cool, store cookies in an airtight container.

These cookies freeze well.

Makes approximately 3 dozen cookies

• BANANA OAT COOKIES •

These cookies are soft and moist, nutritious and high in flavor—perfect for kids' lunch boxes.

⅔ cup uncooked quick-cooking rolled oats
½ cup oat bran
½ cup all-purpose flour
1 teaspoon baking powder
⅛ teaspoon salt
¼ cup unsalted margarine or butter, softened

⅓ cup firmly packed dark brown sugar
2 large egg whites
½ cup mashed very ripe banana (about 1 large)
½ teaspoon vanilla extract
¼ cup chopped pecans
Pecan halves for garnish (optional)

1. Preheat oven to 350°F. Lightly butter two large baking sheets.
2. In a large bowl, stir together oats, oat bran, flour, baking powder, and salt. In another bowl, using a wooden spoon, cream together margarine and sugar until blended. One at a time, add egg whites, beating well after each addition. The mixture may appear curdled. Stir in banana and vanilla. Gradually stir in flour-oat mixture until combined. Stir in chopped nuts.
3. Drop dough by level tablespoonfuls onto prepared baking sheet, leaving about 2 inches between rounds. Flatten slightly, if desired. Top each mound with a pecan half (if desired). Bake one sheet at a time, for 9 to 13 minutes, or until bottoms of cookies are lightly browned.
4. Remove baking sheet to a wire rack and cool for about 2 minutes. Using a metal spatula, transfer cookies to wire racks and cool completely. Repeat baking procedure until all dough is used. When cool, store cookies in an airtight container.

These cookies freeze well.

Makes approximately 2 dozen cookies

◆ CAPPUCCINO CHIP COOKIES ◆

With espresso, cinnamon, and chocolate, these treats taste just like a cup of cappuccino in a cookie.

1¼ cups all-purpose flour
½ teaspoon baking powder
⅛ teaspoon salt
⅛ teaspoon ground cinnamon
½ cup unsalted butter, softened
⅓ cup firmly packed dark brown sugar

⅓ cup granulated sugar
1 large egg
1½ teaspoons instant espresso powder
1 teaspoon vanilla extract
1 cup miniature semisweet chocolate chips
½ cup chopped walnuts

1. In a medium bowl, stir together flour, baking powder, salt, and cinnamon. In a large bowl, using a wooden spoon, cream together butter and sugars, until combined. Stir in egg. In a custard cup, stir espresso powder with vanilla until dissolved. Stir espresso mixture into butter mixture until combined. Gradually stir in flour mixture until blended. Stir in chocolate chips and nuts. Cover and refrigerate dough for 1 hour.

2. Preheat oven to 375°F. Lightly butter two large baking sheets.

3. Drop dough by heaping tablespoonfuls (each cookie should contain about 1½ tablespoons of dough) onto prepared baking sheets, leaving about 2 inches between rounds. Bake one sheet at a time, for 9 to 14 minutes, or until cookies are lightly browned on bottoms.

4. Remove baking sheet to a wire rack and cool for about 3 minutes. Using a metal spatula, transfer cookies to wire racks and cool completely. Repeat until all dough is used. When cool, store the cookies in an airtight container.

These cookies freeze well.

Makes about 2 dozen cookies

◆ CASHEW WHITE CHOCOLATE CHIP COOKIES ◆

These are chocolate chip cookies with a difference—white chocolate and cashew butter.

1¾ cups all-purpose flour
¾ teaspoon baking powder
¼ teaspoon salt
1 cup firmly packed light brown sugar
½ cup unsalted butter, softened
½ cup cashew butter
1 large egg, at room temperature

1 teaspoon vanilla extract
3 ounces white chocolate, coarsely chopped
½ cup unsalted roasted cashews
½ cup chopped pitted dates or raisins
Additional cashews for garnish (optional)

1.   In a medium bowl, stir together flour, baking powder, and salt. In a large bowl, using a wooden spoon, cream together sugar, butter, and cashew butter until blended. Stir in egg until combined. Stir in vanilla. Gradually stir in flour mixture until blended. Stir in white chocolate, cashews, and dates. Cover and refrigerate dough for 30 minutes, or until firm enough to handle.

2.   Preheat oven to 350°F. Lightly butter several large baking sheets.

3.   Shape heaping tablespoons of dough (each cookie should contain about 1½ table-spoons of dough) into balls. Place balls on prepared baking sheets, leaving about 2 inches between balls. Press the balls into rounds 2¼ inches in diameter. Top each round with 2 or 3 of the additional cashews (if desired). Bake one sheet at a time, for 9 to 14 minutes, or until the bottoms of cookies are lightly browned. Remove baking sheet to a wire rack to cool for about 3 minutes. Using a metal spatula, transfer cookies to wire racks and cool completely. Repeat until all dough is used. When cool, store cookies in an airtight container.

Makes approximately 28 cookies

◆ CHERRY CHOCOLATE CHIP COOKIES ◆

The combination of tart dried cherries and chocolate is superb.

1 cup all-purpose flour
½ teaspoon baking powder
¼ teaspoon salt
⅓ cup unsalted butter, softened
⅔ cup firmly packed light brown sugar
1 large egg, at room temperature

½ teaspoon vanilla extract
½ cup tart dried cherries (see Note)
½ cup semisweet or white chocolate chips
*   or ½ cup chopped white chocolate*
*   (about 3 ounces)*
¼ cup slivered blanched almonds

1. In a large bowl, stir together flour, baking powder, and salt. In another bowl, using a wooden spoon, cream together butter and sugar until combined. Stir in egg until blended. Stir in vanilla. Gradually stir in flour mixture until combined. Stir in cherries, chocolate chips, and nuts. Cover and refrigerate dough for 1 hour.

2. Preheat oven to 375°F. Lightly butter two large baking sheets.

3. Drop dough by heaping tablespoonfuls (each cookie should contain about 1½ tablespoons of dough) onto prepared baking sheets, leaving about 2 inches between the cookies. Bake one sheet at a time, for 10 to 12 minutes, or until bottoms of cookies are lightly browned. Remove baking sheet to a wire rack and cool for about 3 minutes. Using a metal spatula, transfer cookies to wire racks and cool completely. Repeat until all dough is used. When cool, store cookies in an airtight container.

These cookies freeze well.

Makes approximately 2 dozen cookies

Note: Dried cherries are often available in gourmet stores, or can be ordered by mail (see page 9). Pitted chopped dates or raisins may be substituted for the dried cherries.

◆ CHEWY COCONUT CHOCOLATE CHIP COOKIES ◆

These cookies are macaroonlike and they have a soft, chewy texture.

¾ cup all-purpose flour
¾ teaspoon baking powder
⅛ teaspoon salt
4 large eggs, at room temperature
¾ cup granulated sugar

1 tablespoon vanilla extract
4 cups sweetened flaked coconut
1½ cups miniature semisweet chocolate
chips

1. Preheat oven to 350°F. Line several large baking sheets with aluminum foil. Lightly butter foil-lined baking sheets, sprinkle with flour, and tap off excess. In a medium bowl, stir together the flour, baking powder, and salt. In a large bowl, using a hand-held electric mixer set at high speed, beat eggs and sugar for 4 to 5 minutes, or until mixture thickens and is light-colored. Beat in vanilla by hand. Using a rubber spatula, stir in flour mixture just until combined. Fold in coconut and chocolate chips.

2. Drop dough by heaping tablespoonfuls (each cookie should contain about 2 table-spoons of dough) onto prepared baking sheets, leaving about 2 inches between the cookies. Bake one sheet at a time, for 15 to 18 minutes, or until edges are just starting to brown. Remove baking sheet to a wire rack and cool for about 10 minutes. Using a metal spatula, transfer cookies to wire racks and cool completely. Repeat until all dough is used. When cool, store the cookies in an airtight container.

Makes approximately 30 cookies

• CHOCOLATE CARAMEL COOKIES •

Swirls of melted chewy caramels are mixed into this chocolaty dough.

*8 ounces semisweet chocolate, coarsely
  chopped*
*2 ounces unsweetened chocolate, coarsely
  chopped*
*24 soft caramels, unwrapped and cut into
  quarters*

1/2 cup unsalted butter, softened
1 cup firmly packed dark brown sugar
2 large eggs, at room temperature
2 teaspoons vanilla extract
1 1/2 cups all-purpose flour
1/4 teaspoon salt

1. Preheat oven to 350°F. Lightly butter several large baking sheets.
2. In the top of a double boiler, over hot, not simmering, water, melt chocolates, stirring occasionally, until smooth. Remove top of double boiler from bottom and cool chocolate for about 10 minutes, or until tepid. In a heavy, medium saucepan, over medium-low heat, melt caramels, stirring constantly, until smooth. Remove pan from heat.
3. In a large bowl, using a hand-held electric mixer, beat butter and sugar until combined. One at a time, beat in eggs, beating well after each addition. Beat in cooled chocolate and vanilla. Beat in flour and salt just until mixed. Drizzle half of the melted caramel over surface of dough and gently fold it into dough. Drizzle remaining caramel over surface and fold it into dough. Drop dough by heaping tablespoonfuls onto prepared baking sheets, leaving about 2 inches between the cookies. Bake one sheet at a time, for 10 to 15 minutes, or until cookies are set. Remove baking sheet to a wire rack and cool for 3 minutes. Using a metal spatula, transfer cookies to wire racks and cool completely. Repeat until all dough is used. When cool, store the cookies in an airtight container.

These cookies freeze well.
Makes approximately 26 cookies

• COLOSSAL COCOA CRINKLES •

These cookies get their rich chocolate flavor from cocoa powder—no need to mess with melting chocolate. They are great dunked in a glass of cold milk. If you want, melt the butter in a large glass bowl in the microwave and you can eliminate using a saucepan.

¾ cup unsalted butter
½ cup unsweetened nonalkalized cocoa
   powder
1 cup granulated sugar
2 cups all-purpose flour
1 teaspoon baking powder

1 teaspoon baking soda
¼ teaspoon salt
2 large eggs, at room temperature, lightly
   beaten
1 tablespoon vanilla extract
Confectioners' sugar

1. In a large saucepan, melt butter. Stir in cocoa powder. Remove pan from heat and stir in sugar. Cool for 10 minutes, or until tepid. In a large bowl, stir together flour, baking powder, baking soda, and salt. Whisk the eggs and vanilla into the butter mixture until combined. Using a wooden spoon, gradually stir in flour mixture until combined. Scrape dough into a bowl and cover and refrigerate for at least 2 hours or overnight.

2. Preheat oven to 350°F. Roll dough into balls 1½ inches in diameter (each cookie should contain about 2 tablespoons of dough). Roll each ball in confectioners' sugar. Place balls of dough on an ungreased baking sheet, leaving at least 2 inches between cookies. Bake for 10 to 15 minutes, or until cookies are set. Remove baking sheet to a wire rack and cool for about 5 minutes. Using a metal spatula, transfer cookies to wire racks and cool completely. Repeat until all dough is used. Store cooled cookies in an airtight container.

These cookies freeze well.

Makes approximately 24 cookies

• ISLAND DREAMIN' COOKIES •

No matter where you are, one bite of these cookies will make you think you are on an island paradise.

2 cups all-purpose flour
½ teaspoon baking powder
½ teaspoon salt
¾ cup unsalted butter, softened
½ cup firmly packed light brown sugar
½ cup granulated sugar
2 large eggs, at room temperature

2 teaspoons vanilla extract
1½ cups jumbo white chocolate chips or
    coarsely chopped white chocolate
1 cup chopped dried papaya
1 cup sweetened flaked coconut
1 cup chopped macadamia nuts

1. In a large bowl, stir together flour, baking powder, and salt. In another bowl, using a hand-held electric mixer set at medium speed, beat butter and sugars for 2 to 3 minutes, or until combined. One at a time, beat in eggs, beating well after each addition. Beat in vanilla. On low speed, gradually beat in flour mixture until combined. Using a wooden spoon, stir in white chocolate, papaya, coconut, and nuts. Cover and refrigerate dough for at least 2 hours or overnight.

2. Preheat oven to 325°F. Using a ¼-cup measuring cup, drop batter by ¼-cupfuls onto an ungreased baking sheet, leaving at least 2 inches between mounds of batter. Bake for 28 to 32 minutes, or until lightly browned. Remove baking sheet to a wire rack and cool for 3 minutes. Using a metal spatula, transfer cookies to wire racks and cool completely. Repeat until all dough is used. When cool, store cookies in an airtight container.

These cookies freeze well.

Makes approximately 20 cookies

• CRANBERRY ORANGE COOKIES •

Try this classic and tangy combination of cranberry and orange studded with chopped pecans.

¾ cup fresh or thawed frozen cranberries
½ cup plus 2 tablespoons granulated sugar
1 cup all-purpose flour
⅓ cup honey-crunch wheat germ
½ teaspoon baking powder
¼ teaspoon salt

½ cup unsalted butter, softened
1 large egg, at room temperature
1 teaspoon vanilla extract
¼ teaspoon grated orange peel
½ cup chopped pecans or walnuts

1. In the container of a food processor fitted with the steel blade, process cranberries and 2 tablespoons of the sugar until finely chopped. Place mixture in a colander and drain for 10 minutes.

2. In a medium bowl, stir together flour, wheat germ, baking powder, and salt. In a large bowl, using a wooden spoon, cream together butter and remaining ½ cup sugar until combined. Stir in egg until blended. Stir in vanilla and orange peel. Gradually stir in flour mixture until combined. Stir in cranberries and nuts. Cover and refrigerate dough for 1 hour, or until firm enough to shape.

3. Preheat oven to 350°F. Lightly butter several large baking sheets. Drop dough by rounded tablespoonfuls (each cookie should contain about 1½ tablespoons of dough) onto prepared baking sheets, leaving about 2 inches between rounds. Flatten mounds slightly. Bake one sheet at a time, for 9 to 14 minutes, or until bottoms of cookies are lightly

browned. Remove baking sheet to a wire rack and cool for 2 minutes. Using a metal spatula, transfer cookies to wire racks to cool completely. Repeat until all dough is used. When cool, store cookies in an airtight container.

Makes approximately 20 cookies

• GINGERED BRANDY SNAPS •

Use your finest china and serve a cup of tea, coffee, or espresso with these delicate lacy cookies.

½ cup all-purpose flour
¼ teaspoon ground ginger
⅛ teaspoon salt
½ cup unsalted butter, cut into
  tablespoons

⅓ cup granulated sugar
2 tablespoons honey
2 tablespoons molasses
1½ tablespoons brandy
½ teaspoon vanilla extract

1. Preheat oven to 350°F. Lightly butter a baking sheet. In a medium bowl, stir together flour, ginger, and salt. In a small saucepan, heat butter, sugar, honey, and molasses until butter melts. Remove pan from heat. Stir in brandy and vanilla. Whisk in flour mixture. Drop 1 teaspoon of batter onto prepared baking sheet. Using the back of a spoon, spread batter in a circular motion to make a 2-inch-diameter round. (If batter becomes too stiff to work with, return saucepan to the stovetop and set on low heat.) Repeat to make 3 more rounds, leaving 3 inches between cookies.

2. Bake for 5 to 7 minutes, or until cookies are golden brown.

3. Remove baking sheet to a wire rack and cool cookies for 1 to 3 minutes, just until set. Working quickly and carefully (see Note), and using a metal spatula, remove one cookie at a time by loosening the sides and turning the cookie over. Working quickly, roll each cookie loosely around the handle of a wooden spoon to form a cylinder that is about ½ to ¾ inch in diameter. Press down on the seam to close the cookie. Cool cookies slightly (15 to 30 seconds) so that they hold their shape before removing from spoon handle to a

wire rack to cool completely. Repeat procedure until all dough is used. Store cooled cookies in an airtight container at room temperature.

Makes approximately 45 cookies

Note: Do not try to prepare more than 4 cookies at once, as they must be rolled quickly before they harden. If cookies harden too quickly, put them back in a hot oven for approximately 1 minute. (If this doesn't work, eat the scraps! As these cookies are delicate, some may break.)

If cookies are underbaked, they will not be crispy when cooled; if cookies are overbaked, they will be difficult to roll.

• LOTS OF CHOCOLATE COOKIES •

These cookies are for chocolate lovers! An extra-rich chocolate dough is filled to the max with chunks of bittersweet and milk chocolate. If you'd like, you can substitute the packaged semisweet and milk chocolate chunks for the chunks called for in the recipe.

3 ounces unsweetened chocolate, coarsely
   chopped
1½ cups all-purpose flour
¼ teaspoon salt
1 cup unsalted butter, softened
1 cup granulated sugar
1 large egg, at room temperature

2 teaspoons vanilla extract
1 cup broken pecans
6 ounces milk chocolate, cut into ½-inch
   pieces
6 ounces bittersweet chocolate, cut into
½-inch pieces

1. Preheat oven to 350°F. In the top of a double boiler, over hot, not simmering, water, melt unsweetened chocolate, stirring occasionally until smooth. Remove top part of double boiler from bottom and cool chocolate for about 10 minutes.

2. In a large bowl, stir together flour and salt. In another bowl, using a hand-held electric mixer set at medium-high speed, beat together butter and sugar. Beat in egg. Beat in cooled chocolate and vanilla. On low speed, beat in flour mixture just until combined.

3. Using a wooden spoon, stir in pecans and chocolate pieces. Drop dough by heaping tablespoonfuls (each cookie should contain about 2 tablespoons of dough) onto ungreased baking sheets, leaving at least 2 inches between the mounds. Bake one sheet at a time, for 8 to 12 minutes, or until cookies are just set. Remove baking sheet to a wire racks and cool for about 5 minutes. Using a metal spatula, transfer cookies to wire racks and cool completely. Repeat until all dough is used. When cool, store cookies in an airtight container.

Makes approximately 32 cookies

• OLD-FASHIONED RAISIN OATMEAL COOKIES •

This recipe is based on one that has been handed down from generation to generation. Plumping the raisins before baking keeps these cookies extra moist.

1 cup raisins
½ cup water
2 cups uncooked old-fashioned rolled oats
2 cups all-purpose flour
1 teaspoon baking powder
¼ teaspoon salt

1 cup unsalted butter, softened
1 cup granulated sugar
2 large eggs, at room temperature
2 teaspoons vanilla extract
1 cup chopped walnuts

1. Preheat oven to 350°F. Lightly butter several large baking sheets.
2. In a small saucepan, combine raisins and water and heat until water begins to boil. Reduce heat and simmer 2 minutes. Remove pan from heat and let raisins cool in the water.
3. In a large bowl, stir together oats, flour, baking powder, and salt. In another bowl, using a wooden spoon, cream together butter and sugar until blended. One at a time, add eggs, stirring well after each addition. Stir in vanilla. Gradually stir in flour-oat mixture until combined. Stir in raisin-water mixture and nuts.
4. Drop dough by heaping tablespoonfuls (each cookie should contain about 1½ tablespoons of dough) onto prepared baking sheets, leaving about 2 inches between mounds of dough. Bake one sheet at a time, for 12 to 15 minutes, or until cookies are lightly browned. Remove baking sheet to a wire rack and cool for about 3 minutes. Using a metal spatula, transfer cookies to wire racks and cool completely. Repeat until all dough is used. When cool, store cookies in an airtight container.

These cookies freeze well.

Makes approximately 4 dozen cookies

◆ ORANGE DATE NUT COOKIES ◆

Dates, nuts, and orange combine with ground rolled oats for a delicious, chewy cookie.

½ cup uncooked old-fashioned rolled oats
1¼ cups all-purpose flour
1 teaspoon baking powder
¼ teaspoon salt
½ cup unsalted butter, softened
⅔ cup firmly packed light brown sugar

1 large egg, at room temperature
1 teaspoon vanilla extract
¼ teaspoon grated orange peel
½ cup chopped pitted dates
½ cup chopped walnuts

1. In the container of a food processor fitted with the steel blade, process rolled oats until ground. In a medium bowl, stir together ground oats, flour, baking powder, and salt. In a large bowl, using a wooden spoon, cream together butter and sugar until combined. Stir in egg until blended. Stir in vanilla and orange peel. Gradually stir in flour mixture until combined. Using a wooden spoon, stir in dates and nuts. Cover and refrigerate dough for 1 hour, or until firm.

2. Preheat oven to 350°F. Lightly butter several large baking sheets. Drop dough by rounded tablespoonfuls (each cookie should contain about 1½ tablespoons of dough) onto prepared baking sheets, leaving about 2 inches between mounds of dough. Flatten the dough slightly. Bake one sheet at a time, for 9 to 13 minutes, or until bottoms of cookies are lightly browned. Remove baking sheet to a wire rack and cool for 2 minutes. Using a metal spatula, transfer cookies to wire racks and cool completely. Repeat until all dough is used. When cool, store cookies in an airtight container.

Makes approximately 25 cookies

• PEANUT BUTTER OATIES •

Chock-full of milk chocolate chips, these cookies are the perfect treat with a glass of ice-cold milk. Try substituting white chocolate or dark chocolate chips for all or some of the milk chocolate chips.

2 cups uncooked old-fashioned rolled oats
1 cup all-purpose flour
1 teaspoon baking powder
1/2 teaspoon salt
1 cup chunky peanut butter
1/2 cup unsalted butter, softened

1/2 cup firmly packed light brown sugar
1/2 cup granulated sugar
3 large eggs, at room temperature
1 tablespoon vanilla extract
2 cups milk chocolate chips
1 1/2 cups shredded coconut

1. Preheat oven to 350°F. In a large bowl, stir together oats, flour, baking powder, and salt. In another bowl, using a hand-held electric mixer set at medium speed, beat peanut butter, butter, and sugars until combined. One at a time, beat in eggs, beating well after each addition. Beat in vanilla. Gradually beat in oat mixture until combined. Using a wooden spoon, stir in chocolate chips and coconut.

2. Drop dough by heaping tablespoonfuls (each cookie should contain about 2 tablespoons of dough) onto an ungreased baking sheet, leaving about 1 inch between mounds of dough. Bake one sheet at a time, for 15 to 18 minutes, or until cookies are lightly browned (the cookies do not spread very much). Remove baking sheet to a wire rack and cool for about 5 minutes. Using a metal spatula, transfer cookies to wire racks and cool completely. Repeat until all dough is used. When cool, store cookies in an airtight container.

These cookies freeze well.

Makes about 4 dozen cookies

◆ SWISS CHOCOLATE CHUNK COOKIES ◆

We think chilling the dough and baking these cookies at a slightly lower than normal temperature makes extra-soft chocolate chunk cookies.

2¼ cups all-purpose flour
¾ teaspoon baking powder
¼ teaspoon salt
1 cup unsalted butter, softened
¾ cup firmly packed dark brown sugar
½ cup granulated sugar

2 large eggs, at room temperature
2 teaspoons vanilla extract
12 ounces Swiss bittersweet chocolate, cut
    into ½-inch pieces
1 cup broken walnuts or pecans

1. In a large bowl, stir together flour, baking powder, and salt. In another bowl, using a wooden spoon, cream together butter and sugars. One at a time, add eggs, stirring well after each addition. Stir in vanilla. Gradually stir in flour mixture until combined. Stir in chocolate and nuts. Cover and refrigerate the dough for at least 2 hours or overnight.

2. Preheat oven to 300°F. Lightly butter several large baking sheets. Drop dough by heaping tablespoonfuls (each cookie should contain about 2 tablespoons of dough) onto prepared baking sheets, leaving at least 2 inches between dough mounds. Bake one sheet at a time, for 20 to 25 minutes, or until cookies are lightly browned. Remove baking sheet to a wire rack and cool for 5 minutes. Using a metal spatula, transfer cookies to wire racks and cool completely. Repeat until all dough is used. When cool, store cookies in an airtight container.

These cookies freeze well.

Makes about 36 cookies

Stuffed Cookies

· CHOCOLATE CITRUS SANDWICHES ·

This cookie offers a classic combination: rich chocolate cookies stuffed with tangy orange cream. For a delicious variation, try these with Chocolate Mint Filling.

COOKIES

1⅓ cups all-purpose flour
⅔ cup unsweetened nonalkalized cocoa powder
½ teaspoon baking soda
¼ teaspoon salt

½ cup unsalted butter, softened
½ cup granulated sugar
¼ cup firmly packed dark brown sugar
1 large egg, at room temperature
1 teaspoon vanilla extract

FILLING

2¼ cups confectioners' sugar
Dash salt
2 tablespoons plus 2 teaspoons orange juice

2 tablespoons heavy (whipping) cream
¼ teaspoon grated orange peel

1. *To prepare cookies:* In a medium bowl, stir together flour, cocoa powder, baking soda, and salt. In a large bowl, using a wooden spoon, cream together butter and sugars until combined. Stir in egg until blended. Stir in vanilla. Gradually stir in dry ingredients. If necessary, knead mixture with your hands until blended. Divide dough into quarters and flatten each quarter into a disk. Wrap each disk in plastic wrap. Refrigerate dough for 1 hour, or until firm enough to roll out.

2. Preheat oven to 350°F. Lightly butter several large baking sheets. Remove one of the disks of dough from refrigerator. Using a rolling pin, roll dough between 2 sheets of

wax paper until it is approximately ⅛ inch thick. Loosen but do not remove top sheet of wax paper from dough. Holding wax paper in place, turn dough over onto an ungreased baking sheet, and remove second sheet of wax paper. Using a 2-inch-diameter cookie cutter, cut cookies from dough, leaving them on the wax paper. Place baking sheet containing wax paper and cookie dough in freezer for 5 to 10 minutes, so that scraps can be easily removed and cut-out cookies can be transferred.

3.   Using a metal spatula, carefully transfer dough cutouts to prepared baking sheets, leaving about 1 inch between cutouts. Bake one sheet at a time, for 8 to 12 minutes, or until cookies are firm. Remove baking sheet to a wire rack to cool for 1 minute. Using a metal spatula, transfer cookies to wire racks and cool completely. Repeat the procedure with remaining chilled dough. Press together dough scraps, form into a disk, and chill if necessary before rerolling; then continue until all dough is used.

4.   *To prepare filling:* In a small bowl, stir together confectioners' sugar and salt. Using a wooden spoon, stir in 2 tablespoons of the orange juice, cream, and orange peel. Add as much of the additional 2 teaspoons of orange juice as needed to make a spreadable filling. (If mixture is too thin, add a little more confectioners' sugar.)

5.   To assemble, spread each of the bottom sides of half of the cookies with about 1½ teaspoons orange filling. Place a second cookie, bottom-side facing down, on top of the filling. Refrigerate cookies for 10 to 15 minutes to set filling. Store cookies in an airtight container.

Makes approximately 28 sandwich cookies

For Chocolate Mint Filling: In the top of a double boiler, over hot, not simmering, water, melt 1 cup mint-flavored chocolate chips with ½ cup heavy (whipping) cream, stirring until smooth. Remove top part of double boiler from bottom and cool chocolate mixture slightly. Refrigerate filling until firm enough to spread. Fill cookies as above, using approximately 1 teaspoon of the chocolate mixture for each cookie sandwich.

For Chocolate-covered Cookies: In the top of a double boiler, over hot, not simmering, water, melt 1 cup semisweet chocolate chips with 2 teaspoons unsalted butter, stirring until smooth. Remove top part of double boiler from bottom and cool chocolate mixture slightly. Using two spoons, dip a well-chilled sandwich cookie into chocolate mixture, turning to coat evenly. Scrape off excess chocolate. Place on a sheet of wax paper and cool for 10 minutes. Repeat procedure with 9 more cookies. Refrigerate cookies for 20 minutes to set coating. Store cookies in refrigerator. Serve at room temperature.

Makes 10 coated cookies

◆ CHOCOLATE CHUNK ICE CREAM SANDWICHES ◆

These cookies stay soft in the freezer because they have a little bit of oil and corn syrup in them. They are also great without the ice cream filling.

2¼ cups all-purpose flour
¾ teaspoon baking powder
¼ teaspoon salt
1 cup unsalted butter, softened
⅔ cup firmly packed light brown sugar
½ cup granulated sugar
2 tablespoons vegetable oil
1 tablespoon light corn syrup

2 large eggs, at room temperature
2 teaspoons vanilla extract
1¾ cups (10-ounce package) milk
    chocolate chunks
1 cup coarsely broken walnuts
5 cups vanilla ice cream (or your favorite
    flavor), softened (see Note)

1. In a large bowl, stir together flour, baking powder, and salt. In another large bowl, using a hand-held electric mixer set at medium speed, beat butter, sugars, oil, and corn syrup for 1 to 2 minutes until combined. One at a time, beat in eggs, beating well after each addition. Beat in vanilla. On low speed, add flour mixture and beat just until combined. Using a wooden spoon, stir in chocolate chunks and walnuts.

2. Preheat oven to 350°F. Lightly butter several large baking sheets. Using a ¼-cup measuring cup, drop dough onto prepared baking sheets, leaving about 3 inches between cookies. Bake for 12 to 17 minutes, or until cookies are lightly browned. Remove baking sheet to a wire rack and cool for about 5 minutes. Using a metal spatula, transfer cookies to wire racks and cool completely. Repeat until all dough is used.

3. To assemble, spread ½ cup softened ice cream on the bottom of one cookie. Place

a second cookie, bottom side facing down, on top of ice cream. Wrap each sandwich individually in plastic wrap and freeze for about 2 hours, or until firm.

Makes 10 ice cream sandwich cookies

Note: Soften ice cream in refrigerator for 30 minutes before using. Alternatively, place ice cream in a microwave oven set at medium (50 percent power) for 20-second intervals until softened.

◆ CHOCOLATE MINT SANDWICH COOKIES ◆

These delicate butter cookies are filled with creamy mint chocolate.

COOKIES
2 cups all-purpose flour
1/4 teaspoon salt
3/4 cup unsalted butter, softened

1 cup granulated sugar
1 large egg, at room temperature
1/2 teaspoon vanilla extract

FILLING
3/4 cup mint-flavored chocolate chips
3 tablespoons heavy (whipping) cream

1 tablespoon unsalted butter

1. *To prepare cookies:* In a medium bowl, stir together flour and salt. In a large bowl, using a wooden spoon, cream together butter and sugar until blended. Stir in egg until blended. Stir in vanilla. Gradually stir in flour mixture until combined. Cover and refrigerate dough for 1 hour, or until firm enough to shape.

2. Shape dough into two 5½-inch-long rolls, each approximately 1½ inches in diameter. Wrap rolls in plastic wrap. Refrigerate rolls for 4 hours, or until firm enough to slice.

3. Preheat oven to 350°F. Lightly butter several large baking sheets.

4. Working with one dough roll at a time, roll dough on a hard surface to reshape. Using a thin, sharp knife, cut dough into approximately ⅛- to ¼-inch-thick slices, so that each roll yields approximately 24 slices. Place slices on prepared baking sheets, leaving about 1½inches between slices. Bake one sheet at a time, for 8 to 12 minutes, or until bottoms of cookies are very lightly browned. Remove baking sheet to a wire rack and cool

for about 2 minutes. Using a metal spatula, transfer cookies to wire racks and cool completely. Repeat until all dough is used.

5. *To prepare filling:* In the top of a double boiler, over hot, not simmering, water, melt chocolate with cream and butter, stirring until smooth. Remove top part of double boiler from bottom and cool chocolate mixture for 10 minutes. Cover and refrigerate filling until firm enough to spread.

6. To assemble sandwiches, spread each of the bottom sides of half of the cookies with approximately 1 teaspoon of chocolate filling. Place a second cookie, bottom side facing down, on top of filling. Refrigerate for 15 minutes to set filling. Store sandwiches in an airtight container.

Makes approximately 24 sandwich cookies

◆ CHOCOLATE RASPBERRY HEART SANDWICHES ◆

These are decorative heart-shaped cookies filled with the classic combination of raspberry and chocolate. Using a small heart-shaped cutter, cut out a "window" in the top cookie to give everyone a peek inside.

COOKIES

½ cup slivered blanched almonds
2 cups all-purpose flour
½ teaspoon baking powder
¼ teaspoon salt

½ cup unsalted butter, softened
⅔ cup firmly packed dark brown sugar
1 large egg, at room temperature
1 teaspoon vanilla extract

FILLING

⅓ cup heavy (whipping) cream
2½ ounces Swiss dark chocolate, chopped

2 to 3 tablespoons seedless raspberry preserves

1. *To prepare cookies:* In the container of a food processor fitted with the steel blade, process nuts until very finely chopped. In a large bowl, stir together flour, baking powder, and salt. In another bowl, using a wooden spoon, cream together butter and sugar until combined. Stir in egg until blended. Stir in vanilla. Gradually stir in flour mixture until combined. Stir in almonds until combined. Cover and refrigerate dough for 2 hours, or until firm enough to roll.

2. Preheat oven to 350°F. Lightly butter several baking sheets. Remove chilled dough from refrigerator and divide into quarters. Form each quarter into a ball. Working with one quarter at a time, roll dough to approximately ⅛-inch thickness between two sheets

of wax paper. Loosen but do not remove top sheet of wax paper from dough. Turn dough over and remove second piece of wax paper. Using a 2¾-inch heart-shaped cookie cutter, cut out cookies from dough. Place wax paper containing dough onto a baking sheet and freeze for 5 to 10 minutes, or until firm enough to handle.

3. Using a metal spatula, carefully transfer cookies to prepared baking sheets, leaving about 1 inch between cookies. Using a ¾-inch heart-shaped cookie cutter, cut out the centers of half the cookies (if desired). Bake one sheet at a time, for 10 to 13 minutes, or until bottoms of cookies are lightly browned. Remove baking sheet to a wire rack and cool for about 1 minute. Using a metal spatula, carefully transfer cookies to wire racks and cool completely. Repeat until all dough is used.

4. *To prepare chocolate filling:* In a small saucepan over medium heat, bring cream to a gentle boil. Remove pan from heat and add chocolate. Let mixture stand for 2 minutes. Stir mixture until smooth and transfer to a small bowl. Cover and refrigerate filling for 30 to 60 minutes, or until firm enough to spread.

5. To assemble, spread bottom sides of completely cooled cookies without the cutout centers with approximately 1 teaspoon of the chocolate filling. Carefully spread bottom sides of the cookies, with cutout centers, with approximately ¼ teaspoon of preserves. Place cutout cookies, preserve-covered side down, on top of chocolate filling. Refrigerate cookies for 10 to 15 minutes to set filling. Store cookies in an airtight container.

Makes approximately 18 sandwich cookies

◆ CREAM CHEESE TURNOVERS ◆

This simple recipe is bound to become a family favorite.

2 cups all-purpose flour
⅛ teaspoon salt
1 cup unsalted butter, softened
1 package (8 ounces) cream cheese,
  softened

¼ cup confectioners' sugar
1 teaspoon vanilla extract
½ cup apricot, strawberry, or pineapple
  preserves

1. In a medium bowl, stir together flour and salt. In a large bowl, using a wooden spoon, cream together butter, cream cheese, and sugar until combined. Stir in vanilla until blended. Gradually stir in dry ingredients until combined. Cover dough and refrigerate for 2 hours, or until firm enough to roll out.

2. Preheat oven to 350°F. Lightly butter several baking sheets. With a lightly floured rolling pin on a lightly floured surface, roll out a quarter of the dough at a time to ⅛-inch thickness. Using a biscuit cutter, cut dough into 3-inch-diameter rounds. (These cookies shrink slightly after cutting and during baking.)

3. Press each round to flatten slightly and top the center of each with approximately ½ teaspoon preserves. Fold dough in half and press edges firmly together to seal. Score rounded edge of each half circle with the tines of a fork. Place half circles on prepared baking sheets, leaving about 1½ inches between crescents. Bake one sheet at a time for 15 to 20 minutes, or until cookies are lightly browned on bottoms. Remove baking sheet to a wire rack to cool for about 3 minutes. Using a metal spatula, transfer cookies to wire rack and cool completely. Repeat baking procedure until all dough is used. When cool, store cookies in an airtight container.

Makes approximately 3 dozen cookies

Note: If these cookies are not completely sealed, some of the preserves may leak onto baking sheets. The preserves are very hot and these "spilled" cookies should be removed carefully. Preserves can be removed from the baking sheets with very hot water.

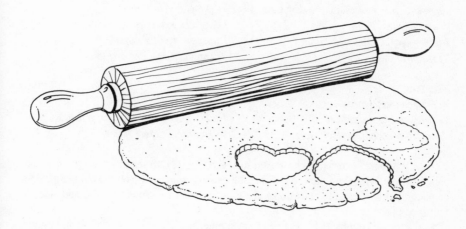

• ESPRESSO CREAM-FILLED BROWNIE SANDWICHES •

These rich, fudgy mocha brownies are delicious on their own; with espresso-flavored cream sandwiched between them, they are heavenly.

BROWNIES

5 ounces Swiss dark chocolate, chopped
1/2 cup unsalted butter
2 large eggs, at room temperature
1/8 teaspoon salt

3/4 cup granulated sugar
1 teaspoon instant espresso powder
1 teaspoon vanilla extract
3/4 cup all-purpose flour

FILLING

1/2 teaspoon hot water
1/4 teaspoon vanilla extract
3/4 teaspoon instant espresso powder

6 ounces cream cheese, softened
1 tablespoon unsalted butter, softened
1/2 cup confectioners' sugar

1. *To prepare brownies:* Preheat oven to 350°F. Lightly butter a 9-inch square baking pan. Line pan with aluminum foil so that foil extends 2 inches beyond two opposite sides of pan. Fold overhanging ends down along outside of pan. Butter bottom and sides of foil-lined pan.

In the top of a double boiler over hot, not simmering, water, melt chocolate and butter, stirring until smooth. Remove top part of double boiler from bottom and cool chocolate mixture to room temperature.

2. In a large bowl, using a hand-held electric mixer set at high speed, beat eggs and salt until foamy. Gradually add sugar, beating for 3 to 4 minutes, or until batter is thick.

In a custard cup, stir together espresso powder and vanilla until dissolved. Beat espresso mixture into egg. Beat in chocolate mixture until blended. Using a wooden spoon, stir in flour until blended.

3. Scrape batter into prepared pan, smoothing top with a spatula. Bake for 30 to 35 minutes, or until a cake tester inserted in center comes out almost clean.

4. Remove pan to a wire rack and let set for approximately 2½ hours, or until completely cool. Using the two ends of the foil as handles, lift brownie "square" out of pan. Invert square onto a flat surface and carefully peel off the foil. Invert again onto a cutting board. Using a long serrated knife, cut into 16 bars, wiping knife clean between each cutting.

5. *To prepare filling:* In a custard cup, stir together water, vanilla, and espresso powder until dissolved. In a medium bowl, using a fork, beat cream cheese and butter until smooth. Beat in espresso mixture. Gradually beat in sugar. Cover filling and refrigerate for 1 hour, or until firm enough to spread.

6. To assemble sandwiches, carefully cut each brownie bar horizontally into two layers using a small serrated knife. Clean knife between each cutting. Top the bottom layer of each brownie with approximately 1 tablespoon of the cream cheese mixture. Place top layer over filling. Refrigerate sandwiches for 15 minutes to set filling. Store sandwiches in a sealed container in the refrigerator.

Makes 16 brownies

For White Chocolate Espresso Filling: In the top of a double boiler, over hot, not simmering, water, melt 3 ounces white chocolate, stirring until smooth. Remove top of double boiler from bottom and stir in 6 ounces softened cream cheese. In a small custard cup, stir together 1 teaspoon instant espresso powder, ½ teaspoon hot water, and ¼ teaspoon vanilla extract until dissolved. Stir into cream cheese mixture. Cover and refrigerate for 1 hour, or until firm enough to spread. Fill brownies as directed above.

• OATMEAL COOKIE SANDWICHES •

These crunchy oatmeal cookies have a choice of creamy peanutty fillings. For peanut butter lovers, double the filling recipes.

COOKIES

1/3 cup sweetened shredded coconut
1 cup all-purpose flour
1/2 teaspoon baking soda
1/4 teaspoon salt
3/4 cup unsalted butter, softened

2/3 cup firmly packed light brown sugar
1 large egg, at room temperature
1/2 teaspoon vanilla extract
2 cups uncooked quick-cooking rolled oats

FILLING

1 cup creamy peanut butter, at room temperature (see Note)
1 tablespoon unsalted butter, softened

1/2 cup confectioners' sugar
1/4 teaspoon vanilla extract

1. *To prepare cookies:* In the container of a food processor fitted with the steel blade, process coconut just until ground. In a medium bowl, stir together flour, baking soda, and salt. In a large bowl, using a wooden spoon, cream together butter and sugar until blended. Stir in egg until combined. Stir in vanilla. Gradually stir in flour mixture until blended. Stir in oats and coconut until combined. Cover and refrigerate dough for 1 hour, or until firm enough to handle.

2. *To prepare filling:* In a medium bowl, using a fork, beat peanut butter and butter until creamy. Beat in sugar and vanilla until smooth. Cover and refrigerate filling for 1 hour to firm slightly.

3. Preheat oven to 350°F. Lightly butter several baking sheets. Shape level tablespoons of dough into balls. Place balls on prepared baking sheets, leaving about 2 inches between balls. Press balls into 2½-inch-diameter disks. Bake for 8 to 12 minutes, or until cookies are lightly browned. Remove baking sheet to a wire rack and cool for 1 minute. Using a metal spatula, transfer cookies to wire racks and cool completely. Repeat until all dough is used.

4. To assemble, spread each of the bottom sides of half of the completely cooled cookies with approximately 1 tablespoon of the peanut butter filling. Place a second cookie, bottom side facing down, on top of filling. Refrigerate sandwiches for 15 minutes to set filling. Store sandwiches in an airtight container in the refrigerator. Serve at room temperature.

Makes approximately 16 sandwich cookies

Note: Use commercially prepared peanut butter for this recipe. Natural peanut butter will make the filling too soft.

For Peanut Butter White Chocolate Filling: In the top of a double boiler over hot, not simmering, water, melt 4 ounces chopped white chocolate with 1 teaspoon unsalted butter. Remove double boiler from heat and stir in ⅔ cup creamy peanut butter and ¼ teaspoon vanilla extract until smooth. Scrape mixture into a small bowl and cool slightly. Cover and refrigerate filling for 30 to 60 minutes, or until firm enough to spread. Fill cookies as above.

• POPPYSEED HAMANTASCHEN •

Hamantaschen are traditionally made for the Jewish festival of Purim. We've filled ours with canned poppyseed filling. You can also use canned prune or apricot filling.

1 can (12½ ounces) poppyseed filling
¾ cup finely chopped walnuts
1½ teaspoons finely grated lemon peel
3 cups all-purpose flour
1 tablespoon baking powder
½ teaspoon salt

½ cup unsalted butter, softened
1 cup granulated sugar
4 large eggs, at room temperature
2 teaspoons vanilla extract
1 teaspoon water

1. Preheat oven to 375°F. In a small bowl, stir together poppyseed filling, walnuts, and lemon peel. In another bowl, stir together flour, baking powder, and salt. Using a hand-held electric mixer set at medium speed, beat butter and sugar until combined. One at a time, beat in 3 of the eggs, beating well after each addition. Beat in vanilla. Stir in dry ingredients until thoroughly combined.

2. Divide dough into twelve equal-sized portions. On a lightly floured surface with lightly floured fingertips, pat out each portion into a circle 4 inches in diameter. If dough is too soft, cover and refrigerate for 15 to 30 minutes. Place a heaping tablespoon of the poppyseed mixture in center of each round. Bend edges of rounds up and in toward the center to form triangles and then pinch raised edges together. Place on ungreased baking sheets, leaving about two inches between triangles. In a small bowl, beat together remaining egg and water. Brush dough portion of each cookie with egg mixture.

3. Bake one sheet at a time, for 20 to 25 minutes, or until cookies are just lightly

browned. Remove baking sheet to a wire rack and cool for 3 minutes. Using a metal spatula, transfer cookies to wire racks and cool completely. Repeat until all dough is used. When cool, store cookies in an airtight container.

These cookies freeze well.

Makes 12 cookies

• RUGULACH •

Try this traditional cookie recipe with a variety of nontraditional fillings.

DOUGH
2½ cups all-purpose flour
¼ teaspoon salt
1 cup unsalted butter, softened
8 ounces cream cheese, softened

½ cup granulated sugar
1 large egg yolk, at room temperature
2 teaspoons vanilla extract

FILLING
⅔ cup granulated sugar
1 tablespoon plus 1 teaspoon ground
   cinnamon

1½ cups finely chopped pecans, walnuts,
   or other nuts
⅔ cup currants or miniature semisweet
   chocolate chips

1. *To prepare dough:* In a medium bowl, stir together flour and salt. In a large bowl, using a hand-held electric mixer set at medium speed, beat butter, cream cheese, and sugar until combined. Beat in egg yolk and vanilla. Gradually beat in flour mixture until blended. Divide dough into quarters and flatten each quarter into a disk. Wrap each disk in plastic wrap and refrigerate for 1 to 2 hours, or until firm enough to roll out. If dough is too firm, let it soften at room temperature for about 5 minutes.

2. *To prepare filling:* In a medium bowl, stir together sugar and cinnamon until combined. Stir in nuts and currants or chips.

3. Preheat oven to 350°F. Lightly butter two baking sheets. Remove one disk of dough from refrigerator. Using a rolling pin, roll dough between two sheets of wax paper until

it forms a circle approximately 9 inches in diameter. Carefully peel off the top sheet of wax paper from dough and replace with another piece of wax paper. Holding the loose piece of wax paper in place, turn dough over onto a baking sheet. Carefully loosen the wax paper now on top, transfer baking sheet to freezer, and chill for 15 minutes. (Because the cream cheese dough is so rich, it is important that you chill the dough.) Sprinkle one-fourth of filling mixture evenly over dough and press it down gently.

4. With a sharp knife, cut the circle into sixteen wedges. Beginning with the outside edge, roll each wedge tightly. Place each rugulach point-side down (so that it does not unroll) on prepared baking sheets, leaving 1 inch between cookies. Prepare remaining rugulach, keeping assembled cookies on the baking sheet in the refrigerator as you work. Bake for 15 to 20 minutes, or until cookies are firm when they are touched lightly with your fingertip.

5. Remove baking sheets to wire racks and cool for about 3 minutes. Using a metal spatula, transfer cookies to racks and cool completely.

Rugulach freezes well.

Makes 64 rugulach

Note: Don't be afraid to experiment with other filling ideas. One possibility is to spread one disk of dough with 2 tablespoons raspberry preserves and then sprinkle the surface evenly with ¼ cup miniature semisweet chocolate chips. Another variation is to spread a disk of dough with 2 tablespoons apricot preserves and then sprinkle the surface with ¼ cup finely chopped pistachios.

Refrigerator, Rolled, and Shaped Cookies

• CINNAMON CREAM CHEESE COOKIES •

Reminiscent of snickerdoodles with the added richness of cream cheese.

COOKIES

1¾ cups all-purpose flour
1¼ teaspoons baking powder
⅛ teaspoon salt
½ cup unsalted butter, softened

4 ounces cream cheese, softened
¾ cup granulated sugar
1 large egg
1 teaspoon vanilla extract

TOPPING

3 tablespoons granulated sugar

½ teaspoon ground cinnamon

1. *To prepare cookies:* In a medium bowl, stir together flour, baking powder, and salt. In a large bowl, using a wooden spoon, cream together butter, cream cheese, and sugar until combined. Stir in egg and vanilla until blended. Gradually stir in flour mixture until combined. Cover and refrigerate dough for 1 to 2 hours, or until firm enough to shape.

2. Preheat oven to 350°F. Lightly butter several large baking sheets.

3. *To prepare the topping:* In a custard cup, stir together sugar and cinnamon.

4. Shape dough into 1-inch-diameter balls. Roll each ball in sugar topping to coat lightly. Place balls on prepared baking sheets, leaving about 2 inches between balls. Bake one sheet at a time, for 10 to 14 minutes, or until bottoms of cookies are just very lightly browned. Remove baking sheet to a wire rack and cool for about 3 minutes. Using a metal spatula, transfer cookies to racks and cool completely. Repeat until all dough is used. When cool, store cookies in an airtight container.

Makes about 45 cookies

• BLACK FOREST COOKIES •

This is a classic combination of cherries and chocolate in a brownielike cookie.

8 ounces Swiss dark chocolate, coarsely
  chopped
2 tablespoons unsalted butter
½ cup all-purpose flour
¼ teaspoon baking powder
⅛ teaspoon salt

¾ cup firmly packed light brown sugar
2 large eggs, at room temperature
1½ teaspoons vanilla extract or kirsch
  (cherry brandy)
¾ cup dried tart cherries (see Note)
⅓ cup milk chocolate chips

1. In top of a double boiler, over hot, not simmering, water, heat dark chocolate and butter, stirring until smooth. Remove top part of double boiler from bottom and cool chocolate mixture for 10 minutes.

2. In a small bowl, stir together flour, baking powder, and salt. In a large bowl, using a hand-held electric mixer set at high speed, beat sugar and eggs for 3 minutes, or until the mixture is light and fluffy. Gradually beat in cooled chocolate mixture. Beat in vanilla. Stir in flour mixture until combined. Stir in cherries and chocolate chips. Cover and refrigerate dough for 20 to 60 minutes, or until firm enough to shape into balls.

3. Meanwhile, preheat oven to 350°F. Lightly butter 2 large baking sheets. Shape cooled dough into approximately 26 balls, each about 1¼ inches in diameter. Place balls on prepared baking sheets, leaving about 2 inches between them. Bake one sheet at a time, for 11 to 15 minutes, or until tops of cookies are just dry and centers are still very moist.

4. Remove baking sheet to a wire rack and cool for about 3 minutes. Using a metal spatula, transfer cookies to wire racks and cool completely. Store cooled cookies in an airtight container.

These cookies freeze well.
Makes approximately 26 cookies

Note: Dried cherries are often available in gourmet stores or can be ordered by mail (see page 9). Pitted chopped dates may be substituted for dried cherries.

• SOFT GINGERBREAD COOKIES •

You can cut this soft, cakey cookie into any shape you'd like. Gingerbread boys and girls are obvious choices. For homecoming or Super Bowl celebrations, cut out football-shaped cookies. Try to bake similar-sized cookies on the same baking sheet. Sprinkle them with sugar, decorate them with cream cheese frosting, or leave them plain.

GINGERBREAD COOKIES
3½ cups all-purpose flour
¾ teaspoon baking soda
½ teaspoon salt
1½ teaspoons ground cinnamon
½ teaspoon ground allspice
½ teaspoon ground ginger
½ teaspoon ground nutmeg
½ teaspoon ground cloves

½ cup unsalted butter, softened
½ cup firmly packed dark brown sugar
½ cup molasses
⅓ cup water
1 tablespoon vanilla extract
Granulated sugar, for sprinkling on
   cookies (optional)

CREAM CHEESE FROSTING (OPTIONAL)
1 cup sifted confectioners' sugar
3 ounces cream cheese, softened

¼ teaspoon vanilla extract
Raisins for decorating

1. *To prepare cookies:* In a large bowl, stir together flour, baking soda, salt, and spices until combined. In another large bowl, using a hand-held electric mixer set at medium speed, beat butter and sugar until combined. Beat in molasses, water, and vanilla. (The mixture will look curdled.) Gradually beat in flour mixture until blended. Divide dough in half and flatten each half into a disk. Wrap each disk in plastic wrap. Refrigerate dough

for 1 to 2 hours, or until firm enough to roll out. If dough is too firm, let it soften at room temperature for about 5 minutes.

2. Preheat oven to 350°F. Lightly butter several baking sheets. Remove one disk of dough from refrigerator. Using a rolling pin, roll dough between two sheets of wax paper until it is approximately ½ inch thick. Transfer dough on wax paper to an ungreased baking sheet and remove top sheet of wax paper. Cut out cookies with cookies cutter or by tracing around cardboard patterns with point of a sharp knife. Place baking sheet containing wax paper and cookie dough in freezer for 3 to 5 minutes so that scraps can be easily removed and cut-out cookies can be transferred. Using a metal spatula, carefully transfer cookies to a prepared baking sheet, leaving about 2 inches between cookies. Sprinkle surface of cookies with granulated sugar (if desired). Bake for 12 to 15 minutes, or until no imprint remains when cookies are touched lightly with your fingertip.

3. Remove baking sheet to a wire rack and cool for about 3 minutes. Using a metal spatula, transfer cookies to racks and cool completely. Repeat procedure with remaining chilled dough. Press together dough scraps, form into a disk, and chill if necessary before rerolling, then continue until all dough is used. (Cookies can be stored in an airtight container in freezer for up to one month and for up to 3 days at room temperature before frosting.)

4. *To prepare frosting:* In a small bowl and using a fork, stir together sugar, cream cheese, and vanilla just until combined and of piping consistency. Add additional sugar or a little milk to achieve the right texture, if necessary. Pipe or frost cookies. Decorate with raisins, if desired.

Makes about 18 cookies (depending on size)

• CHOCOLATE-DIPPED HAZELNUT FINGERS •

These rich cookie fingers studded with chopped toasted hazelnuts and coated in chocolate are elegant enough to serve at a dinner party.

COOKIES

2½ cups cake flour
⅔ cup finely chopped toasted hazelnuts
  (see Note)
¼ teaspoon salt

1 cup unsalted butter, softened
¾ cup granulated sugar
1 large egg, at room temperature
½ teaspoon vanilla extract

CHOCOLATE COATING

5 ounces Swiss dark chocolate, chopped
2 teaspoons unsalted butter

⅓ cup finely chopped toasted hazelnuts

1. *To prepare cookies:* In a medium bowl, stir together flour, nuts, and salt. In a large bowl, using a wooden spoon, cream together butter and sugar until blended. Stir in egg and vanilla until combined. Gradually stir in flour mixture until blended. Cover and refrigerate dough for 2 hours, or until firm enough to handle.

2. Preheat oven to 350°F. Lightly butter several baking sheets. Shape level tablespoons of dough into 2½-inch logs. Place on prepared baking sheets, leaving 1½ inches between cookies. Bake one sheet at a time for 11 to 16 minutes, or until bottoms of cookies are lightly browned. Remove baking sheets to a wire rack to cool for about 3 minutes. Using a metal spatula, carefully transfer cookies to racks and cool completely. Repeat until all dough is used.

3. *To prepare chocolate coating*: In the top of a double boiler, over hot, not simmering, water, heat chocolate and butter, stirring until melted. Remove pan from heat. Dip the end of each cooled cookie into chocolate to coat approximately ⅓ of each cookie with glaze. Dip chocolate-coated tips of each cookie into the nuts for the coating. Place cookies on a wax-paper-lined baking sheet and refrigerate for 10 to 15 minutes, or just until chocolate hardens.

Makes approximately 3½ dozen cookies

Note: To toast and skin hazelnuts, spread them in a single layer on a baking sheet and bake at 350°F. for 10 to 15 minutes, shaking the sheet a couple of times, or until nuts are lightly browned under their skins. Wrap nuts in a clean kitchen towel and cool completely. Place nuts in a sieve and rub them against the sieve to remove skins. Place toasted nuts in the container of a food processor fitted with the steel blade. Process until finely chopped. (You will need 1 cup of hazelnuts for this recipe.)

• CHOCOLATE-DUNKED PEANUT BUTTER COOKIES •

Peanut butter and chocolate make one of America's favorite flavor combinations. These peanut butter cookies are dipped in chocolate and then in chopped peanuts.

1½ cups all-purpose flour
½ teaspoon baking powder
⅛ teaspoon salt
¾ cup chunky peanut butter
¼ cup unsalted butter, softened

⅔ cup firmly packed light brown sugar
2 large eggs, at room temperature
2 teaspoons vanilla extract
1 cup semisweet chocolate chips
1⅓ cups finely chopped peanuts

1. In a medium bowl, stir together flour, baking powder, and salt. In a large bowl, using a hand-held electric mixer set at medium-high speed, beat peanut butter, butter, and sugar until combined. One at a time, beat in eggs, beating well after each addition. Beat in vanilla. On low speed, beat in flour mixture just until combined.

2. Place two 15-inch-long pieces of plastic wrap on a work surface. Divide dough in half and scrape one half each into the centers of the pieces of plastic wrap. Form each half into a roll approximately 1½ inches in diameter and 9 inches long. Wrap the plastic wrap tightly around the rolls of dough and refrigerate or freeze for 1 to 2 hours, or until firm enough to cut into slices. (If desired, the rolls of dough can be kept frozen for up to 1 month. Thaw dough in refrigerator overnight before baking.)

3. Preheat oven to 350°F.

4. Working with one roll at a time, roll dough back and forth on a hard surface to reshape. Using a thin, sharp knife, cut dough into ¼-inch-thick slices and place them on an ungreased baking sheet, leaving 1 inch between slices. (If dough crumbles when

you slice it, allow it to stand at room temperature for a few minutes.) Bake for 8 to 12 minutes, or until when a cookie is pressed with your fingertip, a slight imprint remains. Remove baking sheet to a wire rack to cool for about 5 minutes. Using a metal spatula, transfer cookies to wire racks and cool completely. Repeat until all dough is used.

5.   In the top of a double boiler, over hot, not simmering, water, melt chocolate chips, stirring occasionally, until smooth. Remove top part of double boiler from bottom and cool chocolate for about 10 minutes, or until tepid. Dip cooled cookies into chocolate, using a small knife or spatula, if necessary, to coat approximately half of each cookie with glaze. Immediately dip cookies into peanuts and place them on waxed paper until chocolate hardens. (If it is warm, place cookies in refrigerator for a few minutes to set the chocolate.) Store cookies in an airtight container with wax paper between layers.

Makes about 50 cookies

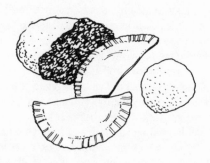

• CHOCOLATE HAZELNUT SANDIES •

These buttery, chocolaty cookies are easy to make and combine the delightful duo of chocolate and hazelnuts. They would also be delicious with another type of nut, such as pecans.

4 ounces unsweetened chocolate
1 cup unsalted butter, softened
1¼ cups confectioners' sugar
1½ teaspoons vanilla extract

2 cups all-purpose flour
¼ teaspoon salt
1 cup toasted hazelnuts, coarsely chopped
  (see Note)

1. In the top of a double boiler, over hot, not simmering, water, melt chocolate, stirring occasionally, until smooth. Remove top part of double boiler from bottom and cool chocolate for about 10 minutes, or until tepid. In a large bowl, using a wooden spoon, cream together butter and sugar. Beat in cooled chocolate and vanilla. Beat in flour and salt just until mixed. Stir in hazelnuts.

2. Place a 24-inch-long piece of plastic wrap on a work surface. Scrape dough into center of plastic wrap and form it into a roll approximately 2 inches in diameter and 16 inches long. Wrap plastic tightly around roll and refrigerate or freeze for 1 to 2 hours, or until firm enough to slice. (If desired, the roll of dough can be kept frozen for up to 1 month. Thaw dough in refrigerator overnight before baking.)

3. Preheat oven to 350°F. Roll dough back and forth on a hard surface to reshape. Using a thin, sharp knife, cut dough into ½-inch-thick slices and place them on an ungreased baking sheet, leaving 2 inches between slices. (If dough crumbles when you slice it, allow it to stand at room temperature for a few minutes.) Bake for 12 to 16 minutes, or until when pressed with your fingertip, a slight imprint remains. Remove baking sheet

to a wire rack until completely cool. Repeat until all dough is used. Using a metal spatula, transfer cookies to an airtight container.

These cookies freeze well.

Makes about 32 cookies

Note: To toast and skin hazelnuts, spread them in a single layer on a baking sheet and bake at 350°F. for 10 to 15 minutes, shaking the sheet a couple of times, or until nuts are lightly browned under their skins. Wrap nuts in a clean kitchen towel and cool completely. Place nuts in a sieve and rub them against the sieve to remove skins.

While many of us make cut-out cookies around the holidays, you won't want to save these cookies for a once-a-year experience. There's a recipe for frosting, but they are delicious plain. Sprinkle them with granulated or colored sugar before baking, if you don't plan on frosting them.

CUT-OUT COOKIES

2½ cups all-purpose flour
½ teaspoon salt
1 cup unsalted butter, softened

½ cup granulated sugar
1 large egg, at room temperature
1 tablespoon vanilla extract

FROSTING

Approximately 2 cups sifted confectioners'
  sugar
¼ cup unsalted butter, softened

½ teaspoon vanilla extract
1 to 2 tablespoons milk
Liquid or paste food coloring (optional)

1. *Prepare the cookies:* In a medium bowl, stir together flour and salt. In a large bowl and using a wooden spoon, beat butter and sugar until combined. Stir in egg. Stir in vanilla. One-third at a time, stir in flour mixture just until thoroughly mixed. Divide dough in half and flatten each half into a disk. Wrap each disk in plastic wrap and refrigerate for 1 to 2 hours, or until firm enough to roll. If the dough is too firm, let it soften at room temperature for about 5 minutes.

2. Preheat oven to 375°F. Remove one disk of dough from refrigerator. Using a rolling pin, roll dough between two pieces of wax paper until it is approximately ¼ inch thick. Transfer dough on wax paper to an ungreased baking sheet and remove top sheet of wax

paper. Cut out cookies with cookies cutters or by tracing around cardboard patterns with the point of a sharp knife. Place baking sheet containing wax paper and cookie dough in freezer for 3 to 5 minutes so that scraps can be easily removed and cut-out cookies can be transferred. Using a metal spatula, carefully transfer cookies to another baking sheet, leaving about 1 inch between cookies. Bake for 8 to 10 minutes, or just until cookies are starting to brown lightly around edges.

3. Remove baking sheet to a wire rack and cool for about 5 minutes. Using a metal spatula, transfer cookies to racks and cool completely. Repeat procedure with remaining chilled dough disk. Press together dough scraps, form into a disk, and chill if necessary before rerolling, then continue until all dough is used. (Cookies can be stored in an airtight container in freezer for up to one month and for up to 3 days at room temperature before frosting.)

4. *To prepare frosting:* In a large bowl and using a hand-held electric mixer set at low speed, beat together sugar, butter, and vanilla until it reaches spreading consistency. Add additional sugar or a little milk, if necessary, to achieve the right texture. Add food coloring, if desired. Pipe or frost cookies with frosting.

Makes about 36 cookies (depending on size)

• DATE NUT PINWHEELS •

A delectable date and nut mixture forms a spiral in these yummy cookies. Grated orange peel adds a little extra pizzazz.

2 cups all-purpose flour
½ teaspoon baking powder
¼ teaspoon salt
½ cup unsalted butter, softened
¾ cup granulated sugar, divided
½ cup firmly packed light brown sugar
1 large egg, at room temperature

1½ teaspoons vanilla extract
1 pound (about 3½ cups) chopped pitted dates
¾ cup orange juice
¼ teaspoon grated orange peel (optional)
1 cup chopped walnuts

1. In a medium bowl, stir together flour, baking powder, and salt. In a large bowl, using a hand-held electric mixer set at medium speed, beat together butter, ½ cup of the granulated sugar, and brown sugar until combined. Beat in egg and vanilla. Beat in flour mixture until smooth. Cover dough and refrigerate for 2 hours or overnight.

2. Meanwhile, make date and nut filling: In a medium saucepan, combine dates, orange juice, remaining ¼ cup sugar, and orange peel (if desired). Cook over medium heat for 4 to 6 minutes, or until thick, stirring constantly. Remove pan from heat and cool to room temperature. Stir in walnuts.

3. With a lightly floured rolling pin on a lightly floured work surface, roll out one-half of dough into a 12-by-9-inch rectangle, a scant ¼ inch thick. Spread half the filling evenly over dough. Starting with a 12-inch side, roll up the dough like a jelly roll. Wrap dough with wax paper, so the seam of the roll is on the bottom. Repeat with remaining dough and filling. Chill rolls until firm.

4. Preheat oven to 375°F. Lightly butter several baking sheets.

5. Working with one dough roll at a time, roll dough back and forth on a hard surface to reshape. Using a thin, sharp knife, cut dough into slices a generous ¼ inch thick. Transfer slices to prepared baking sheets, leaving about 2 inches between slices. Bake one sheet at a time, for 8 to 12 minutes, or until lightly browned. Remove baking sheet to a wire rack to cool for about 3 minutes. Using a metal spatula, transfer cookies to wire racks and cool completely. Repeat until all dough is used. When cool, store cookies in an airtight container.

These cookies freeze well.

Makes about 60 cookies

◆ LEMON SESAME COOKIES ◆

These buttery cookies are coated with toasted sesame seeds.

2 cups all-purpose flour	1 large egg, at room temperature
1 teaspoon baking powder	1 tablespoon fresh lemon juice
1/4 teaspoon salt	1 teaspoon vanilla extract
1/2 cup unsalted butter, softened	1/4 teaspoon grated lemon peel (see Note)
1/3 cup granulated sugar	1 cup toasted, hulled sesame seeds (see
1/3 cup firmly packed light brown sugar	Note)

1. In a medium bowl, stir together flour, baking powder, and salt. In a large bowl, using a wooden spoon, cream together butter and sugars until blended. Stir in egg, lemon juice, vanilla, and lemon peel until combined. The mixture may have a curdled appearance. Gradually stir in flour mixture until blended. Cover and refrigerate the dough for 2 hours, or until firm enough to shape.

2. Preheat oven to 375°F. Lightly butter several baking sheets. Place sesame seeds in a pie plate. Shape dough into balls 1¼ inches in diameter. Press balls into sesame seeds to coat, flattening balls into 2-inch rounds. Turn rounds over and press the other side into sesame seeds to coat.

3. Place dough rounds on prepared baking sheets, leaving about 1 inch between rounds. Bake one sheet at a time, for 10 to 13 minutes, or until bottoms of cookies are lightly browned. Remove baking sheet to a wire rack and cool for about 3 minutes. Using a metal spatula, transfer cookies to wire racks and cool completely. Repeat until all dough is used. When cool, store cookies in an airtight container.

These cookies freeze well.

Makes approximately 26 cookies

Note: Grated orange peel may be substituted for the lemon peel and orange juice for the lemon juice.

To toast sesame seeds, spread in a large skillet and cook over moderate heat, stirring often, for 3 to 4 minutes, or until lightly browned. Remove from skillet and cool.

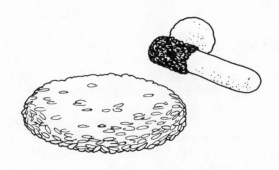

• MACADAMIA NUT RUSKS •

These cookies are baked twice for an extra crunch.

2 cups all-purpose flour
2 teaspoons baking powder
⅛ teaspoon salt
⅔ cup unsalted butter, softened
⅔ cup granulated sugar

2 large eggs, at room temperature
1 teaspoon vanilla extract
¼ teaspoon grated lemon peel (optional)
⅔ cup finely chopped lightly salted
   macadamia nuts

1. In a medium bowl, stir together flour, baking powder, and salt. In a large bowl, using a wooden spoon, cream together butter and sugar until blended. One at a time, add eggs, stirring well after each addition. Stir in vanilla. Stir in lemon peel (if desired). Gradually stir in flour mixture until combined. Stir in nuts. Cover and refrigerate dough for 1 hour, or until firm enough to shape.

2. Shape dough into two 6-inch-long rolls, each approximately 1¾ inches in diameter. Wrap rolls in plastic. Refrigerate rolls for 3 hours, or until firm.

3. Preheat oven to 350°F. Lightly butter two large baking sheets. Working with one dough roll at a time, roll dough back and forth on a hard surface to reshape. Place dough rolls on one of the prepared baking sheets, leaving 6 inches between rolls. Bake for 22 to 27 minutes, or until bottoms of rolls are lightly browned and tops are dry. Reduce oven temperature to 275°F. Remove baking sheet to a wire rack and cool for 5 minutes. Using a pancake turner, transfer rolls to wire rack and cool for 20 minutes.

4. Transfer rolls to a cutting board. Using a large serrated knife and with a sawing motion, slice rolls into ½-inch-thick slices. The slices may still be slightly doughy. Lay slices on the other large baking sheet, leaving about ½inch between slices. Bake for 20

minutes. Using a small metal spatula, turn cookies over. Bake for 20 to 25 minutes more, or until cookies are lightly browned.

5.   Remove baking sheet to a wire rack and cool for about 2 minutes. Using a metal spatula, transfer cookies to wire racks and cool completely. When cool, store cookies in an airtight container.

Makes approximately 26 cookies

Based on the mascot of the Chi Omega sorority, these cleverly shaped two-tone sugar cookies appeal to young and old alike.

2 cups all-purpose flour
1 teaspoon baking powder
1/4 teaspoon salt
1/2 cup unsalted butter, softened
1 cup granulated sugar

1 large egg, at room temperature
2 teaspoons vanilla extract
2 ounces semisweet chocolate, melted
36 chocolate chips
18 whole cashews

1. In a medium bowl, stir together flour, baking powder, and salt. In a large bowl and using a hand-held electric mixer set at medium speed, beat butter and sugar together until combined. Beat in egg. Beat in vanilla. One-third at a time, beat in flour mixture just until thoroughly mixed. Transfer one cup of dough to a medium bowl and stir in melted chocolate until blended. Wrap chocolate dough and vanilla dough in separate plastic sheets and freeze for 15 to 30 minutes, or until doughs are firm enough to hold their shapes.

2. Shape the chocolate dough into a 12-inch-long roll approximately 1¼ inches in diameter. Using a rolling pin, roll vanilla dough between two pieces of wax paper to a 12-by-5½-inch rectangle. Remove the top sheet of wax paper. Place roll of chocolate dough in center of vanilla dough. Using wax paper as a support, wrap vanilla dough around chocolate roll and seal the seam together. (If the doughs become too soft to work with, refrigerate or freeze them until they are firm enough to hold their shapes.) Freeze wrapped roll for 30 to 60 minutes, or until firm enough to slice.

3. Preheat the oven to 350°F. Lightly butter two baking sheets.

4.   Roll dough back and forth on a hard surface to reshape. Using a thin sharp knife, cut roll into slices ⅓ inch thick. Place two slices next to each other on a baking sheet and press them together so that they are joined to each other. Using your fingertips, pinch together the two top outside edges of vanilla dough to form ears. Place a chocolate chip on each of the dark circles of dough and place a cashew where the slices meet at the bottom to form a nose. Leaving 2 inches between cookies, continue making the rest of the owls. Bake one cookie sheet at a time for 10 to 15 minutes, or until top edges of cookies are very lightly browned. Cool cookies on baking sheet on a wire rack for about 3 minutes. Using a metal spatula, transfer cookies to racks and cool completely. Store cookies in an airtight container at room temperature.

These cookies freeze well.

Makes approximately 18 cookies

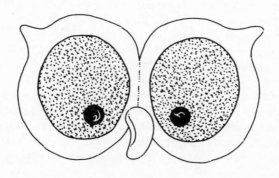

• CHOCOLATE BEARS •

These rich chocolate cookies with whimsical trim make a wonderful treat for kids.

1 cup unsalted butter, softened
1⅓ cups firmly packed dark brown sugar
1 large egg, at room temperature
1 teaspoon vanilla extract
½ teaspoon salt
1 tablespoon water

2 tablespoons unsweetened nonalkalized cocoa powder
2 ounces unsweetened chocolate, melted and cooled
3 cups all-purpose flour, divided
½ teaspoon baking soda
Red paste food color

1. In a large bowl and using a wooden spoon, cream together butter and sugar until blended. Stir in egg until combined. Stir in vanilla and salt. Remove ⅓ cup of butter mixture to a small bowl.

2. Add water to remaining butter mixture in large bowl, stirring until combined. Add cocoa powder, stirring until blended. Stir in chocolate until combined. Stir in 2½ cups flour and baking soda until combined.

3. To the ⅓ cup butter mixture, stir in remaining ½ cup flour until blended. Remove ¼ cup of this vanilla dough to a custard cup. To remaining vanilla dough, add a small amount of red paste food color, until dough is a bright red color. Cover and refrigerate all the dough for 4 hours, or until chocolate dough is firm enough to roll out.

4. Preheat oven to 350°F. Lightly butter several large baking sheets. Reserve 3 tablespoons of chocolate dough for decorating. On a lightly floured surface, with a lightly floured rolling pin, roll out one-quarter of the chocolate dough to a thickness of ³⁄₁₆ inch. Using a 4½-inch-long bear-shaped cookie cutter (see Note), cut out bears. Transfer dough

bears to a prepared baking sheet. Repeat the procedure with remaining chilled chocolate dough. Press together chocolate dough scraps and chill, if necessary, before rerolling; continue until all chocolate dough is used.

5.   To decorate each bear (using illustration as a guide): Flatten 2 small balls (3/16 inch in diameter) of vanilla dough and place on the bear's face to create 2 cheeks that are just touching. Form 2 eyes by flattening 2 smaller balls of vanilla dough and place them on the bear's face. Create eyeballs with tiny bits of chocolate dough placed in the center of each eye. Make the nose by shaping a small piece of chocolate dough into a triangle with a rounded top, and place it in the center of the cheeks. Form a tongue with a small amount of red dough and place it under the cheeks. Using the red dough, form a heart and/or bow tie for the bear. (An aspic cutter can be used to cut out the hearts.) Place bow tie on cookie slightly under tongue and place heart on one side of bear's chest. Repeat the procedure until all bears are decorated. Leftover dough can be formed into circles and baked.

6.   Bake one sheet at a time, for 12 to 14 minutes, or until tops of cookies are dry and firm. Remove baking sheet to a wire rack and cool for about 5 minutes. Using a metal spatula, carefully transfer cookies to wire racks and cool completely. When cool, store cookies in airtight container.

These cookies freeze well.

Makes approximately 18 cookies

Note: If you do not have a bear cookie cutter, photocopy the bear pattern on page 100. Cut it out and trace the pattern onto firm cardboard. Cut out pattern. Using the point of a small sharp knife, trace the bear outline into the dough.

Teatime
Temptations

◆ CHOCOLATE PEANUT BUTTER CREAM ROLL-UPS ◆

These delicate cookie rolls are stuffed with a peanut butter cream and then dipped in dark sweet chocolate to create an elegant dessert. Also try them with Hazelnut Chocolate Filling.

COOKIES
½ cup cake flour
⅓ cup confectioners' sugar
Dash salt

¼ cup unsalted butter, melted and cooled
2 large egg whites, at room temperature
½ teaspoon vanilla extract

CHOCOLATE COATING
4 ounces Swiss dark chocolate

2 teaspoons unsalted butter

PEANUT BUTTER FILLING
1 cup heavy (whipping) cream, chilled
¼ cup confectioners' sugar

¼ cup smooth peanut butter, at room temperature
¼ teaspoon vanilla extract

1. *To prepare cookies:* Preheat oven to 375°F. Generously butter several baking sheets. Dip the edge of a 3-inch cookie cutter or glass into additional flour. Press cookie cutter onto a baking sheet to make a circle outline. Repeat the process so you have 3 circles on each sheet, leaving 3 inches between circles.

2. In a small bowl, stir together flour, sugar, and salt. In another bowl, using a fork, beat together butter, egg whites, and vanilla until blended. Stir in flour mixture until smooth. Drop dough by heaping teaspoonfuls (each cookie should contain about 1½ teaspoons of dough) into the center of each circle. Spread dough within floured outlines on baking sheet. Bake for 4 to 5 minutes, or until edges of cookies are just lightly browned.

3. Place baking sheet on open oven door. Working quickly and carefully (see Note), and using a metal spatula, remove one cookie at a time by loosening the sides. Place cookie bottom-side up on a clean potholder or cloth kitchen towel. Working quickly, roll each cookie loosely around a wooden spoon handle to form a cylinder about ½ to ¾ inch in diameter. Press down on the seam to close the cookie. Cool cookies slightly (15 to 30 seconds) so that they hold their shape, before removing from spoon handle to wire racks to cool completely. Repeat procedure until all dough is used.

4. *To prepare chocolate coating*: In the top of a double boiler, over hot, not simmering, water, heat chocolate and butter, stirring until melted. Remove pan from heat. Dip an end of each cooled cookie into chocolate to coat approximately ½ of each cookie with coating, spreading evenly with a small spatula. Place cookies on a wax paper–lined baking sheet. Refrigerate for 10 to 15 minutes, or just until chocolate hardens.

5. *To prepare filling*: Immediately before serving, in a small bowl, using a hand-held electric mixer, beat cream, sugar, peanut butter, and vanilla until stiff peaks form. Place mixture in a pastry bag fitted with a ¼-inch-diameter plain tip. Pipe cream filling into prepared cookie rolls. Refrigerate until serving time. These cookies are best prepared the day of serving.

Makes approximately 21 cookies

Note: Do not try to prepare more than 3 cookies at once, as they must be rolled quickly before they harden. If cookies harden too quickly, put them back in a hot oven for approximately 1 minute. (If this doesn't work, eat the scraps! As these cookies are delicate, some may break.)

If cookies are underbaked, they will not be crispy when cooled; if cookies are overbaked, they will be difficult to roll.

Once these cookies are filled, they must be served immediately as the filling makes the cookies soggy.

For Hazelnut Chocolate Filling: Immediately before serving, in a small bowl, with a hand-held electric mixer, beat ¾ cup heavy (whipping) cream with ⅓ cup hazelnut chocolate spread (such as Nutella) until stiff peaks form. Fill cookies as directed.

• FORTUNE COOKIES •

It's lots of fun to personalize the messages that you put in these cookies and make them extra special. Make sure to have everything ready before baking these, as speed is essential.

⅓ cup all-purpose flour
2 tablespoons cornstarch
⅛ teaspoon salt
¼ cup unsalted butter, softened

¼ cup granulated sugar
2 large egg whites, at room temperature
½ teaspoon vanilla extract
¼ teaspoon almond extract

1. Cut out 15 strips of paper, each about 3 by ½ inches, and write (with a ballpoint pen) a different fortune on each strip. Preheat oven to 350°F. Lightly butter a large baking sheet. Dip the edge of a 3-inch cookie cutter or glass into additional flour. Press cookie cutter onto prepared baking sheet to make a circle outline. Repeat process so you have 4 circles on sheet, leaving 2 inches between circles.

2. In a small bowl, stir together flour, cornstarch, and salt. In a medium bowl, using a hand-held electric mixer set at medium-high speed, beat butter and sugar until combined. Beat in egg whites and extracts until smooth. Beat in flour mixture. Drop dough by level tablespoonfuls into center of each circle. With a small spatula, spread dough within floured outlines on the baking sheet. Bake for 5 to 8 minutes, or until edges of cookies are just lightly browned.

3. Place baking sheet on open oven door. Working quickly and carefully (see Note), and using a metal spatula, remove one cookie at a time by loosening the sides. Place cookie bottom-side up on a clean potholder or cloth kitchen towel. Put one of the fortunes in center of cookie and fold cookie in half without creasing it. While holding the two side edges of the cookie together, carefully draw cookie gently down over the rim of a glass to

crease it in half. Place the cookie in a muffin pan cup to hold its shape until cool. Repeat this procedure to make remaining cookies.

Makes 15 cookies

Note: Do not try to prepare more than 4 cookies at once as they must be rolled quickly before they harden. If cookies harden too quickly, put them back in a hot oven for approximately 1 minute. (If this doesn't work, eat the scraps! As these cookies are delicate, some may break.)

If cookies are underbaked, they will not be crispy when cooled; if cookies are overbaked, they will be difficult to roll.

• MELT-IN-YOUR-MOUTH SUGAR COOKIES •

Based on a Swedish recipe, these light and ultra-delicate cookies will simply melt away as soon as you take a bite. A plate of these, accompanied by fresh fruit and an assortment of cheeses, would be a refined and welcome ending to a big meal.

2 cups sifted all-purpose flour
2 tablespoons granulated sugar plus
   approximately ½ cup sugar
Dash salt
1 cup unsalted butter, chilled

⅓ cup heavy (whipping) cream
½ teaspoon vanilla extract
Approximately ½ cup granulated sugar
   for dipping the cookies

   1. In a large bowl, stir together flour, 2 tablespoons of the sugar, and salt. Cut butter into ½-inch cubes and distribute them over flour mixture. Using your fingertips, quickly press butter cubes into flour mixture until combination resembles coarse meal. In a small bowl, stir together cream and vanilla. Add cream mixture to flour mixture and stir to combine. Cover and refrigerate dough for 2 hours or overnight.

   2. Preheat oven to 375°F. Put remaining ½ cup sugar in a flat dish or pie plate. With a lightly floured rolling pin on a lightly floured work surface, roll out one third of the dough to a ⅛-inch thickness. (Keep unused dough in refrigerator.) Cut out cookies with a round cookie cutter 2½ inches in diameter. Transfer rounds to sugar and turn so that both sides are thoroughly coated. Place rounds on an ungreased baking sheet, leaving about 1 inch between them. Prick each round 4 times with tines of a fork. Bake for 7 to 9 minutes, or until cookies are just beginning to brown slightly around the edges. Remove baking sheet to a wire rack to cool for 3 minutes. Using a metal spatula, transfer cookies to wire racks and cool completely. Repeat until all dough is used. When cool, store cookies in an airtight container.

   These cookies freeze well.
Makes about 50 cookies

• PISTACHIO SNOWBALLS •

These confections, a variation of Mexican wedding-cake cookies, are chock-full of chopped pistachio nuts and a hint of almond. Of course, you could always use the classics—walnuts or pecans.

⅔ cup lightly salted, shelled pistachio nuts
2⅓ cups cake flour
⅛ teaspoon salt
1 cup unsalted butter, softened

1½ cups confectioners' sugar, divided
½ teaspoon vanilla extract
¼ teaspoon almond extract

1.   Place nuts in container of a food processor fitted with the steel blade. Process until very finely chopped.

2.   In a medium bowl, stir together flour and salt. In a large bowl, using a wooden spoon, cream together butter and ½ cup confectioners' sugar until blended. Stir in extracts until combined. Gradually stir in dry ingredients until blended. Stir in nuts. Cover and refrigerate dough for 2 hours, or until firm enough to handle.

3.   Preheat oven to 375°F. Lightly butter several baking sheets. Shape dough into balls 1 inch in diameter. Place balls on prepared baking sheets, leaving about 1 inch between them. Bake one sheet at a time for 10 to 15 minutes, or until tops of cookies are set and bottoms are lightly browned. Meanwhile, place remaining cup of confectioners' sugar in a pie plate. Remove baking sheet to a wire rack and cool for about 2 minutes. Carefully remove cookies and immediately dip the warm cookies into sugar to coat. Cool cookies on wire racks. Sprinkle cooled cookies with any remaining sugar. Repeat until all dough is used. When cool, store cookies in an airtight container. Handle these cookies carefully as they are very delicate.

These cookies freeze well.

Makes approximately 4 dozen cookies

◆ TRULY VANILLA WAFERS ◆

Two real vanilla beans are used to add an extra-rich, robust vanilla flavor to these delicate wafers.

2 vanilla beans
⅓ cup heavy (whipping) cream
2¼ cups all-purpose flour
½ teaspoon baking powder
⅛ teaspoon salt

1 cup unsalted butter, softened
¾ cup granulated sugar
1 large egg, at room temperature
2 teaspoons vanilla extract

1. Using the point of a sharp knife, split vanilla beans. Scrape the seeds into a small saucepan. Add cream and vanilla beans and bring mixture to a boil. Remove pan from heat and let mixture stand for 15 minutes. Remove beans, squeezing them of all their liquid (see Note).

2. Preheat oven to 350°F. In a medium bowl, stir together flour, baking powder, and salt. In another bowl, using a hand-held electric mixer set at medium speed, beat together butter and sugar until combined. Beat in egg until blended. Beat in cream mixture and vanilla extract. Gradually beat in flour mixture until combined.

3. Drop dough by heaping teaspoonfuls onto an ungreased baking sheet, leaving about 2 inches between each mound. Bake for 7 to 9 minutes, or until cookies are just beginning to brown lightly around the edges. Remove baking sheet to a wire rack to cool for about 3 minutes. Using a metal spatula, transfer cookies to wire racks and cool completely. Repeat until all dough is used. When cool, store cookies in an airtight container.

These cookies freeze well.

Makes about 60 cookies

Note: You can rinse the beans with warm water and let them dry for several hours at room temperature. Store dry beans in a container of granulated or confectioners' sugar. The sugar will absorb the aromatic flavor within a couple of days and give you vanilla-flavored sugar.

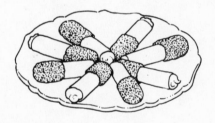

Create Your Own Cookies

Cookies lend themselves well to lots of variations. Indeed, you can modify many of the preceding recipes. For example, if chocolate chips, dried fruit, or chopped nuts are stirred into the batter of cookies, you can usually substitute an equal amount of your choice of similar additions for a new version of the cookie. Or, split the batter in half and add different chips, nuts, or dried fruits to each half to get two types of cookies from each batch.

For our sandwich cookies, you can easily substitute the filling from another cookie recipe, although you might have to adjust the amount of filling. Or dip a corner of stuffed or unstuffed cookies in melted chocolate. Or try the sandwich cookies without their fillings.

Let the following simple cookie recipe and guidelines be your springboard for making your own signature cookie creations. If you substitute whole wheat flour or rolled oats for a small part of the all-purpose flour, the texture of the cookies will change.

Trial and error is the best way to determine what you like and what works well. Dried fruits, nuts, spices, chocolate chips, or chopped chocolate can be varied to come up with interesting combinations.

BASIC COOKIES

1¼ cups all-purpose flour
½ teaspoon baking powder
⅛ teaspoon salt
½ cup to 10 tablespoons unsalted butter,
  softened (see Note)

½ cup granulated sugar
1 large egg, at room temperature
1 teaspoon vanilla extract
¾ to 1¼ cups "additions" of your choice

1. Preheat the oven to 350°F. Lightly butter two large baking sheets.
2. In a medium bowl, stir together flour, baking powder, and salt. In a large bowl, using a wooden spoon, cream together butter and sugar until blended. Stir in egg and vanilla until combined. Gradually stir in flour mixture until blended. Stir in additions

such as chips, chopped dried fruits, or nuts. Cover and refrigerate dough for 1 hour, or until firm enough to hold its shape.

Drop dough by heaping tablespoonfuls (each cookie should contain about 1½ tablespoons of dough) onto prepared baking sheets, leaving about 2 inches between each dough mound. Flatten dough slightly. Bake one sheet at a time, for 9 to 15 minutes, or until cookies are lightly browned on bottoms. Remove baking sheet to a wire rack and cool for about 3 minutes. Using a metal spatula, transfer cookies to wire racks and cool completely. Repeat until all dough is used. When cool, store cookies in an airtight container.

Makes about 21 cookies

Note: Using 10 tablespoons butter will produce crisper, richer cookies.

The yield will vary slightly depending on the amount of additions such as chips and nuts. This recipe can be doubled.

SUBSTITUTIONS

FLOUR

- For up to ½ cup all-purpose flour, substitute an equal amount of whole wheat flour.
- For ¼ cup all-purpose flour, substitute ½ cup uncooked quick-cooking or old-fashioned rolled oats.

SHORTENING

- Unsalted margarine may be substituted for butter.
- ¼ cup peanut butter may be substituted for ¼ cup butter. If using 10 tablespoons butter, 6 tablespoons peanut butter can be substituted for 6 tablespoons butter (¼ cup plus 2 tablespoons). To incorporate the peanut butter, cream it into the butter.

SWEETENER

- For granulated sugar, substitute an equal amount of firmly packed light or dark brown sugar. Or use half firmly packed brown sugar and half granulated sugar.

ADDITIONS

Stir in up to 1¼ cups total of the following per recipe:

FRUIT

- Raisins, and chopped *dried* fruits such as pitted dates, prunes, apricots, pineapple, pears, peaches, cranberries, cherries, and apples

NUTS

- Peanuts, cashews, pine nuts, shelled pistachio nuts, or chopped nuts such as almonds, pecans, walnuts, hazelnuts, macadamia nuts, Brazil nuts, and mixed nuts (baking nuts on a cookie sheet at 350°F. for 5 to 7 minutes, or until golden, will add a toasted flavor)

MISCELLANEOUS

- Assorted sizes of chips (miniature to jumbo) in a variety of flavors—white chocolate, mint-flavored chocolate, semisweet, milk chocolate, peanut butter or butterscotch (try a combination of flavors)
- Assorted chocolate bars such as Swiss dark chocolate or white chocolate, chopped into chunks

EXTRACTS, SPICES, AND FLAVORINGS

Add extra flavor to the dough by mixing in these ingredients in the amounts listed:

- ¼ teaspoon almond, rum, brandy, or maple extract
- ⅛ teaspoon ground cinnamon, ground allspice, cloves, ginger, mace, or nutmeg— or a combination of spices
- ¼ teaspoon grated orange or lemon peel
- 1 teaspoon instant espresso powder or instant coffee dissolved in a teaspoon of vanilla extract
- up to 2 tablespoons toasted sesame seeds
- up to ¼ cup shredded or flaked sweetened coconut

CHOCOLATE

- For chocolate cookies, stir 2 or 3 ounces semisweet chocolate, melted and cooled, into butter and sugar mixture. Don't add melted chocolate to recipes in which you have already used peanut butter.

Index